Mid-Atlantic
Trout Streams
and Their Hatches

Other Books by Charles R. Meck

Fishing Small Streams with a Fly Rod
Great Rivers—Great Hatches (with Greg Hoover)
Meeting and Fishing the Hatches
Pennsylvania Trout Streams and Their Hatches
Patterns, Hatches, Tactics, and Trout

Mid-Atlantic Trout Streams
and Their Hatches

*Overlooked Angling in Pennsylvania,
New York, and New Jersey*

Charles R. Meck
with Bryan C. Meck and D. Craig Josephson

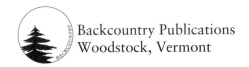

Backcountry Publications
Woodstock, Vermont

An Invitation to the Reader

With time, access points may change, and road numbers, signs, and landmarks referred to in this book may be altered. If you find that such changes have occurred near the streams described in this book, please let the author and publisher know so that corrections may be made in future editions. Other comments and suggestions are also welcome. Address all correspondence to:

Fishing Editor
Backcountry Publications
PO Box 748
Woodstock, Vermont 05091

Library of Congress Cataloging-in-Publication Data
Meck, Charles R.
Mid-Atlantic trout streams and their hatches : overlooked angling in Pennsylvania, New York, and New Jersey / Charles R. Meck with Bryan C. Meck and D. Craig Josephson.
    p.   cm.
Includes index.
ISBN 0-88150-397-5 (alk. paper)
1. Trout fishing—Middle Atlantic States—Guidebooks. 2. Fly fishing—Middle Atlantic States—Guidebooks. 3. Aquatic insects—Middle Atlantic States. 4. Middle Atlantic States—Guidebooks. I. Meck, Bryan C. II. Josephson, D. Craig. III. Title.
SH688.U6M425   1997
799.1'757—dc21
                                                            97-10386
                                                                CIP

Published by Backcountry Publications
A division of The Countryman Press
PO Box 748
Woodstock, VT 05091

Distributed by W.W. Norton & Company, Inc.
500 Fifth Avenue
New York, NY 10110

Text design by Rachel Kahn
Cover design by Susan Wheeler
Cover photograph of Ron Payne fishing Harveys Creek by Charles R. Meck
Interior photographs by Charles R. Meck, unless otherwise noted
Maps by Paul Woodward, © 1997 The Countryman Press
Fly illustration on chapter opening pages by Tammy Hiner

Printed in the United States of America
10 9 8 7 6 5 4 3 2 1

To my wife, Shirley, and my children, Lynne and Bryan, and my grand-children, Lauren and Matthew. Thanks for your encouragement.
—Charles Meck

To my dad—my teacher, my mentor, my friend.
—Bryan Meck

To my grandfather, Silvio Benigni, for giving me the heritage of fly-fishing; to my friend Charlie Meck for sharing his knowledge; and to my wife, Lisa, for her patience in my pursuit of trout.
—D. Craig Josephson

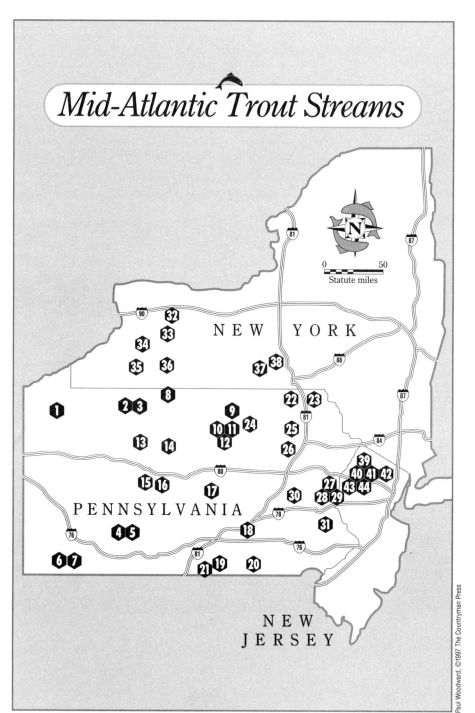

Mid-Atlantic Trout Streams

NEW YORK

PENNSYLVANIA

NEW JERSEY

0   50
Statute miles

(See pages 168–169 for New Jersey's Streams)

Contents

AKNOWLEDGMENTS

A book discussing 44 trout streams and rivers and their hatches in three states isn't just the work of one person. Many have contributed to this book in significant ways. Because many of the overlooked streams see few fly-fishers, Bryan Meck, Craig Josephson, and I had to search for local experts. On streams that no one fly-fished regularly, it meant going back to their banks on three, four, or five occasions to verify the hatches.

In eastern Pennsylvania we had help from Joe DeMarkis and Todd Seigfried on Bear Creek. Al Dally and Rich Keesler helped on Martins Creek; Rich also helped me locate some anglers for New Jersey rivers. Jim Misuira of Collegeville set up the trip to the Manatawny. Ron Payne in Lehman took me on fishing trips to Harveys, Tunkhannock, and Starrucca Creeks. Don Baylor of Stroudsburg helped me with McMichael and Pocono Creeks near his hometown. George Smith helped me with Schrader Creek just southwest of Towanda.

In the western third of Pennsylvania, Len Lichvar and Randy Buchanan of the Johnstown area fished with me on Bens Creek. Ron Dorula, Mark DeFrank, and Eugene Gordon of the Uniontown area fished with me on Dunbar Creek. Eugene Gordon keeps a diary of the hatches on that stream and shared his list with me. Ken Haddix of Conneaut Lake helped on Woodcock Creek by checking temperatures throughout the summer and by fishing with me on the stream for a day. Dave Kitchen fished with me on Potato and Marvin Creeks, and Ron German helped me with the hatches in the northwest. Paul Miller fished with me on Big Meadow Run and a tributary, Beaver Creek.

In the north-central area of the Keystone State, Charlie Pierce spent a day fly-fishing with me on the Tioga River. In south-central Pennsylvania, Frank Angelo fished with me on Middle Creek, and Dick Getz helped me with the hatches.

In New Jersey I had a lot of help. Thanks go first to John Roetman and the East Jersey Chapter of Trout Unlimited, who helped locate anglers to fish with me on the Rockaway River. George Slack was a great help on the Pequest and Paulinskill Rivers. Kevin Wnuck took a couple of days off and fished with me on the Big Flat Brook and the Pequest, Musconetcong, and Raritan Rivers. Aaron and Sam Sandus of the Hacklebarney Chapter of Trout Unlimited, Randy Brockway of the Natural Resources Conservation Service, and Chris Testa of the Morris County Soil Conservation District aided immensely. Mark Dettmar also fished with me for a day on the Big Flat Brook.

In New York, Scott Cornett, Jim Pomeroy, and Al Himmel assisted on Wiscoy Creek and the Genesee River. Bob Herson aided on the Oatka. Paul Roberts fished and discussed the hatches on the East and West Branches of the Owego.

Thanks also to Cortland Line Company, the Orvis Company, and Toyota. I field-tested the new Toyota RAV 4 for a week while I traveled to some of the streams. It's one of the finest four-wheel drives I've ever used. Thanks to Orvis for letting me test a Trident fly-rod—it truly is one of a kind.

Finally, thanks to my son, Bryan Meck, and my friend Craig Josephson for covering 11 of the streams we discuss in the book. They fished those streams, checked the hatches, and wrote about their experiences.

Mid-Atlantic
Trout Streams
and Their Hatches

I.

Introduction

Another book on northeastern trout streams? The market already has four books covering all or part of Pennsylvania's trout streams, several books on New York trout fishing, and at least one on New Jersey's cold water. Do we need another book on the subject? Before you say no, let's look at part of the problem.

In the past few years, significant changes have occurred in trout fishing in the Northeast. Sections of many of the tristate area's top streams have gone private. Top-notch streams like Big Fishing Creek near Lock Haven in Pennsylvania have experienced unbelievable increases in fishing pressure.

Yellow Creek in southwestern Pennsylvania is another example of angling pressure. Recently Paul and Pat Antolosky and I fly-fished the delayed-harvest area. When we parked we counted 10 other cars in the lot. When we fished the special-regulations water, we counted 15 anglers fishing the water. We hiked the entire 1-mile section of regulated water and saw not one open pool.

In mid-May I traveled to the Slate Run Tackle Shop to autograph books. That weekend Craig Josephson and I fly-fished the famous and productive Slate Run. As we drove I began counting the cars parked along this freestone stream. There were 25 in a 5-mile stretch. We were heading for a section of water just below the Cushman Branch and traveled the last mile on a narrow, rutted, rocky dirt road. When we arrived at a bridge over this small stream, we spotted seven cars parked there. As we hiked upstream a half mile from the bridge, Craig and I counted more than a half-dozen anglers. Needless to say, we caught few trout on that small, crowded water.

Add a hatch to some of the East's fine streams and the pressure will almost certainly increase. When the green drake comes to Yellow, Penns, and Big Fishing Creeks, the Little Juniata River, the Delaware River, or the Beaverkill, you'll see firsthand what overcrowding can do to the serene setting you expect when trout fishing. Hundreds of anglers come to these streams to match the hatch. It's almost a carnival atmosphere on Penns Creek when the green drake appears.

When that same green drake hatch appears on Big Fishing Creek, you'll find literally hundreds of anglers on the narrows section looking for a place to fish. I vividly remember one hatch on Big Fishing Creek when I finally had to give up looking for a place to fly-fish in disgust. This excessive pressure has increased many anglers' concerns that more and more landowners will begin posting sections of the stream.

Hatches other than the green drake can cause heavy fly-fishing pressure, too. Fish Spring Creek in central Pennsylvania during the sulphur hatch in late May, and you'll share the water with unbelievable numbers of fly-fishers. Or take a look at Yellow Breeches in south-central Pennsylvania when the whitefly appears in mid-August: In the catch-and-release area, anglers will be shoulder to shoulder.

But the problem isn't limited to Pennsylvania. Drive along New York's fabled Beaverkill and count the anglers. The number rose so high a decade

A rainbow caught on a Pheasant Tail Bead Head Nymph on the East Branch of the Antietam (see chapter 21)

or so ago it turned me off to fly-fishing on this great trout stream. Add a hatch to the Beaverkill or the Willowemoc and you'll see even more fly-fishers in action.

And this overcrowding problem isn't restricted to the United States. I recently fly-fished Ontario's Grand River with Don Bastian, Rick Whorwood, Jim Richardson, and James Morozzo. One morning in late August I counted five cars parked at the upper end of the river. Each morning we fished we tried to arrive before 6—we had to, to get there before other fly-fishers arrived. The few trout I caught on the river had hook marks all over their mouths.

To me, one of the most important elements of fly-fishing is solitude. You don't get much of that anymore on Pennsylvania's Yellow Breeches or Big Fishing Creeks or on the other streams and rivers I've mentioned. You do, however, get privacy on many of the streams in this book. Recently, on a 5-day trip to streams like the Tioga River, Pleasant Stream, Rock Run, and Roaring Branch, I fished in complete privacy—I did not see one other angler. Now that's fly-fishing the way I like it! One weekend in early July when I fly-fished the West Branch of the Genesee River, two cars stopped so their drivers could ask me why I was fishing so late in the season. Neither had seen an angler on the stream in the past month.

I've already alluded to how we can reduce this serious overcrowding on our more famous streams: Either diminish the number of fly-fishers or let anglers know about other choices. We can't do much about the first option—in fact, the number of fly-fishers continues to grow enormously. So the only solution is to let anglers know about other viable fly-fishing waters.

Look at Baker Run in Clinton County and Wallace Run in central Pennsylvania's Centre County as typical examples. While you'll find dozens of anglers fishing nearby Young Womans Creek, you'll likely have Baker Run to yourself. While hundreds of anglers vie for space during the sulphur hatch on Spring Creek, you'll find plenty of room fishing the same hatch on Wallace Run. And both Wallace and Baker Runs hold good hatches. No, you won't experience hatches as heavy as those of Spring or Big Fishing Creeks—but neither will you encounter the hordes of anglers.

The greatest pleasure fly-fishing gives me is communication with nature. I enjoy fly-fishing in a quiet, isolated setting—and on many of the streams we've included in this book you can still do that! Look at Rock Run in north-central Pennsylvania. Once you travel along this magnificent, swift, freestone stream, you'll want to come back again and again. Each time I return, I stand in awe of the huge waterfalls and deep pools that Rock Run has carved on its way downstream to its meeting with

*An angler fishes while a hendrickson hatch appears
on the Raritan River (see chapter 44).*

Lycoming Creek. At one spot, the stream might be 20 or 30 feet wide. In the next, huge ledges might constrict it to 10 feet.

But there's more to this book than just overlooked Pennsylvania trout streams. Recently I talked to a group of young anglers and conservationists about the great trout rivers of the US. By the way, that weeklong workshop, the brainchild of Jack Beck, Inky Moore, and Pennsylvania Trout Unlimited, should help produce an educated new generation of fly-fishers. At my talk I showed several slides of a trout stream and asked the group where they thought it was located. Several yelled out "Montana." "Colorado," shouted several others. When I told them the photos had been taken in Ken Lockwood Gorge on the South Branch of the Raritan River—in New Jersey—they were shocked. I showed them photos of other New Jersey rivers, like the Big Flat Brook. They all looked on in deepening amazement at what New Jersey has to offer fly-fishers. Surprisingly, New Jersey has a lot of great trout waters—many of them underrated by anglers. We've included six rivers that may be of interest to you. Although these waters certainly aren't overlooked, they are underrated.

Craig Josephson recently took me to the East and West Branches of Owego Creek, along with the Wiscoy and East Koy Creeks. These southern-tier New York streams don't receive nearly the angling pressure that the Beaverkill and Willowemoc do. Yet all of these lesser-known streams hold great hatches and plenty of streambred trout. Spend a day on these southern New York streams in late May or June and you'll find few other anglers. There are seven important New York southern-tier streams in this book.

Yes, on the majority of streams we've included here you'll have little competition from other anglers. The one difficulty Bryan Meck, Craig Josephson, and I have had in preparing this book is finding fly-fishers who regularly frequent many of them. They are so overlooked that few anglers know the actual hatches on them. The three of us had to return to the streams many times to verify the hatches ourselves. If you see an unlisted hatch on one of these streams or rivers, please notify us through the publisher—we'll update the book for its next printing.

NOTES FOR USING THIS GUIDE

STREAMS INCLUDED IN THE BOOK

You'll find 31 Pennsylvania, 7 New York, and 6 New Jersey streams here. I visited a lot more than that, but I felt that many of them didn't contain either good trout water, trout, or hatches. Bryan Meck wrote about Manada, Otter, Antietam, Oatka, and Conewago Creeks. Craig Josephson fished and wrote about the other New York trout streams and rivers. I've added Bryan's or Craig's name to the streams each wrote about.

RATING THE STREAMS

To further help you decide whether or not you want to fish a stream, we have rated each one listed in the book. Yes, our scale is subjective, but you might find it useful. Have you ever wondered how one stream or river stands up against another? How do the hatches compare with those on nearby streams? What about the quality of the water and trout? Will you find streambred browns or rainbows and native brookies? How about the environment through which the stream flows? Is it along a busy road or highway—or will you find this particular trout stream in an isolated, scenic spot? All of these factors add up to making that fishing trip worthwhile and memorable. That's why we've come up with our scale. We used the following ratings:

1. Don't even tell your worst enemy.
2. Don't bother getting your waders wet.
3. It's worth a quick look.
4. Spend a couple of hours on this one.
5. It has some good hatches.
6. It has some good hatches and streambred trout.
7. It has some great hatches and trout all season long.
8. Hatches are outstanding and there are plenty of streambred trout.
9. Fish this one many times.
10. Quit work immediately and go fishing on this stream.

So which streams make my rating of 10? Big Fishing Creek (Clinton County), Penns Creek, Spring Creek, and the Delaware River are 10s. Streams like the lower Bald Eagle, Oswayo Creek, and the Little Juniata River I would assign a rating of 9. All of my 9- or 10-ranked streams are included in *Pennsylvania Trout Streams and Their Hatches*, a companion to this volume.

Which streams made the highest rating in this book? Overlooked streams and rivers like Beaverdam Creek in Pennsylvania; the South Branch of the Raritan River and the Big Flat Brook in New Jersey; and Wiscoy, West Branch Owego, and Oatka Creeks in New York we've rated as 7s.

DELORME MAP PAGE NUMBER

For each stream in Pennsylvania, New York, and New Jersey we've listed the page number in the DeLorme Mapping Company's *Pennsylvania* and

*New York Atlas and Gazetteer*s where that stream can be found. Because there's not yet a DeLorme atlas to New Jersey, the page numbers in the New Jersey section of this book refer to Pennsylvania maps.

POSITIVES AND NEGATIVES

For each stream included in the book we've listed "Positives" and "Negatives"—quick glimpses of some of the good and bad points about the stream you plan to fly-fish. Is it small? Is it difficult to fly-fish? We've probably listed these as negatives. Many of our streams in Pennsylvania have problems with acid mine drainage, too. Some are barely able to support any mayfly or trout populations. We've listed that as a negative where applicable.

On the other hand, does the stream boast spectacular scenery? That's part of the total experience for me. You'll probably find that listed as a positive. To me, hatches and streambred trout make a stream special. If one of the streams we've included in this book features these, then it's one I prefer fishing. And of course trout fishing is all about cold water. If the stream holds cold water all summer long this is certainly a bonus. Fishing over native brook trout always gives me a thrill. We've given streams with native trout populations a positive.

Even the Grand River in Ontario has crowded conditions.

AN OVERVIEW OF THE STREAMS

Do you want a quick glimpse of all of the streams and rivers included in the book? Would you like to see where they're located, what the best hatches are, whether they contain streambred trout? The table on page 21 shows all of this and more.

TROUT

What kind of trout will you encounter on your trips? Some streams have native (N) or brook trout; some have streambred (Sb) brown or rainbow trout; and some streams hold just stocked (S) or holdover (H) trout. Those containing streambred and native trout have been rated higher than those with just stocked or planted trout. Both native and streambred are wild trout.

SIZE OF STREAM

Is the stream or river you plan to fly-fish a small (S), medium (M), or large (L) one? Of course, the upper section of a stream will generally be smaller than its lower end.

BEST TIME TO FLY-FISH

Is the stream noted for its fly-fishing in spring (E, for early)? Does it hold a lot of midseason (M) hatches like the blue-winged olive dun and the slate drake in late May and early June? Or will you see rising trout and hatches like the trico and whitefly late (L) in the season? Of course, the better the stream, the more likely you are to see good fly-fishing and hatches all through the season.

BEST HATCH

This heading is very subjective, but here we list those hatches that seem to be most dependable and heaviest on each stream. The South Branch of the Raritan River in New Jersey holds a great sulphur hatch. We've listed that here. Pocono Creek in northeastern Pennsylvania hosts a spectacular blue-winged olive dun hatch in late May and early June. You'll find that hatch listed in the table, too.

Have an enjoyable trip through the book and remember, it's up to you to prevent overcrowding on many of our streams—by enjoying and fly-fishing the overlooked and underrated streams of the mid-Atlantic. Remember, too, that it's important to always return the trout you've caught to the stream.

Stream or River	Type of Trout	Size of Stream	Best Time to Fish	Best Hatches	Rating	Location
PENNSYLVANIA						
1. Woodcock Creek	S	S to M	E, M	Cream cahill	4	NW
2. Marvin Creek	S, Sb, H	M	E, M	Sulphur	5	NW
3. Potato Creek	S, Sb, N, H	M to L	E, M	Hendrickson	6	NW
4. Bens Creek	S, Sb, N, H	S to M	E, M	Quill gordon	5	SW
5. Beaverdam Creek	S, Sb, H	S	M, L	Sulphur, trico	7	SW
6. Dunbar Creek	S, N, H	M	M, L	Olive stonefly	5	SW
7. Big Meadow Run	S, H, Sb	M	E, M	Sulphur	5	SW
8. Genesee River	S, Sb, N, H	S to L	E, M	Sulphur	6	NC
9. Tioga River	S, N	M	E, M	Hendrickson	6	NC
10. Roaring Branch	S, H, N, Sb	S	E, M	Early brown stonefly	6	NC
11. Rock Run	N, S	S	E, M, L	Quill gordon	6	NC
12. Pleasant Stream	S, Sb, N, H	S to M	E, M, L	Quill gordon	7	NC
13. Medix Run	S, N	S	E, M	Blue quill, quill gordon	5	NC
14. Baker Run	S, Sb, N	S	E, M	Blue quill	6	NC
15. Black Moshannon Creek	S	M	E, M	Light cahill	4	NC
16. Wallace Run	S, Sb, N	S	E, M	Blue quill, quill gordon	5	NC
17. Middle Creek	S, Sb, N	S to L	E, M	Sulphur, slate drake	6	SC
18. Manada Creek	S, Sb, H, N	S to M	E, M	Sulphur	6	SC
19. Conewago Creek	S	S to M	E, M	Sulphur	5	SC
20. Otter Creek	S, Sb	S	E, M	Sulphur	4	SC
21. Antietam Creek	S, Sb	M	E, M, L	Sulphur	6	SC
22. Snake Creek	S, H	M	E	Hendrickson	4	NE
23. Starrucca Creek	Sb, N, H, S	M	E, M	Hendrickson	6	NE
24. Schrader Creek	S, N	M	M, L	Stoneflies	5	NE
25. Tunkhannock Creek	S, Sb, N, H	S, M, L	E, M	Hendrickson	5	NE
26. Harveys Creek	S, H, Sb	M	E, M	Sulphur	7	NE
27. Pocono Creek	Sb, H, S, N	M	E, M, L	Blue-winged olive dun	7	NE
28. McMichael Creek	Sb, H, S	M	E, M	Blue-winged olive dun, slate drake	5	NE
29. Martins Creek	S, Sb, H	M	E, M, L	Sulphur	6	SE
30. Bear Creek	S, H, N	S	E, M	Hendrickson, sulphur	5	SE
31. Manatawny Creek	Sb, N, H, S	M	E, M, L	Hendrickson, trico, whitefly	6	SE
NEW YORK						
32. Oatka Creek	Sb, S, H	M	E, M	Hendrickson	7	NW
33. East Koy	Sb, H, S	M	E, M	Caddis	6	W
34. Wiscoy Creek	Sb, S	M	E, M, L	Hendrickson, green drake	7	W
35. Ischua Creek	S, Sb, H	S to M	M, L	Sulphur, green drake	5	SW
36. Genesee River	H, S	L	E, M	Hendrickson, trico	6	SC
37. West Branch Owego	Sb, N	S	E, M	Blue-winged olive dun	7	C
38. East Branch Owego	Sb, H, S, N	M	E, M	Hendrickson, slate drake, trico	6	C
NEW JERSEY						
39. Big Flat Brook	S, Sb, H, N	S to M	E, M, L	Slate drake, sulphur	7	NW
40. Paulinskill River	H, S	L	E, M	Sulphur	5	NW
41. Pequest River	H, S	M	E, M, L	Light cahill	6	NW
42. Rockaway River	H, S	S to M	E, M	Light cahill	5	N
43. Musconetcong River	Sb, H, S	M to L	E, M, L	Tan caddis	6	NW
44. South Branch Raritan	S, Sb, N, H	M to L	E, M, L	Slate drake, sulphur	7	W

II.

Hatches

Art Gusbar of Somerset, Pennsylvania, called me in late May 1996 with a perplexing question: "What happened to all the sulphurs this year?" Art fished four times on the Little Juniata River in central Pennsylvania in mid- and late May and saw a total of one sulphur dun emerge. What had happened to the hatches? By mid-June dozens more fly-fishing friends had also called to ask what was going on.

Steve Sywensky of Lemont, Pennsylvania, owner of Fly Fishers' Paradise, laments the paucity of hatches on some central Pennsylvania trout streams he fished in the summer of 1996. He feels the Little Juniata River suffered most. Steve and Walt Young—Walt is a noted fly-tier—also say that they've seen few slate drakes and fewer sulphurs than normal on this river.

Russ Mowry of Latrobe, Pennsylvania, has fly-fished on Pine Creek near Slate Run for decades. His 1996 trip to that stream was a disaster: A good day was one when he or his fishing buddy caught more than three trout. I stood on Pine Creek one evening in early June from 8 until well past dark, and I saw one trout rise. In this same stretch and on this same early-June day a decade ago I would have seen between 50 and 100 trout rising. On that 1996 evening, too, I saw maybe a half-dozen sulphurs emerge. I *did* witness a great spinner flight of coffin flies and brown drakes—but in the time I waited not one of these spinners fell onto the surface.

Russ Mowry had experienced the same frustration just a couple of nights before. He'd stood on the same section of Pine Creek two nights in a row and didn't see one spinner land on the surface. Russ said that as far as he knows, the drakes are still moving upstream. What has happened to the hatches on many streams throughout the region?

A male Sulphur Spinner works well when Paraleptophlebia *species emerge.*

Kim Falkowski of the Fly Fishing Shop in Far Hills, New Jersey, may have the answer. The snowmelt and flooding that occurred on January 19, 1996, had an incredible effect on the streams of the East—Pennsylvania's, New York's, and New Jersey's. Kim didn't see any consistent hatch all through the whole summer of 1996. He too blames the floods in January at least for some of this inactivity. Paul Roberts lives near Ithaca, New York, and he feels that New York streams have also been affected. Paul believes that stoneflies and *Isonychia* nymphs survived the intense flooding better than others.

You can see for yourself what happened by making a kick sample check for insects in a stream. Just kick a small section of the bed and see how many aquatic insects you dislodge.

I recently talked to a landowner along Honey Creek near Lewistown, Pennsylvania, who had a startling revelation. Shortly after that January flood, the air temperature dropped by 30 degrees. When this landowner surveyed the damage to his property that afternoon after the flood near the now-falling stream, he found dozens of crayfish frozen on the shoreline. What do you think happened to the mayflies on this same stream? Multiply this effect by thousands and you can readily see what effect the January flood had on the season's hatches. On streams where I saw heavy sulphur hatches years before I saw diminished ones in 1996. Free swimmers seemed to have suffered most from the flood. Burrowing mayflies seemed least affected.

Still, the flood may not have been all bad. Steve Young feels that the sulphur and trico hatches on Spring Creek appeared in heavier numbers than usual in 1996. Why? He feels that much of the polluted substrate in Spring Creek got washed away. That makes sense, doesn't it?

It took area streams and rivers several years to recover from Hurricane Agnes and its flooding in 1972. This latest incident could end up affecting streams for nearly that long.

NEW HATCHES

Have I found any important hatches in preparation for this book that I didn't find when I wrote *Pennsylvania Trout Streams and Their Hatches* in 1993? Did some seem more common than I'd originally thought? The answer is yes. I found the gray drake *(Siphlonurus quebecensis)* appearing on many more streams than I'd first realized. Almost every stream of northwestern Pennsylvania has great hatches of this species around the end of May. Look for the spinners to appear above fast-water stretches around 7 PM.

The same goes for the green drake on eastern waters. These huge mayflies frequent many more streams than I originally thought. New York streams like Wiscoy Creek host good green drake hatches in early June.

We all know about the early blue quill that usually appears the last two weeks in April on most regional streams. But I found other, similar hatches that emerged later in the season. On many streams and rivers I found late-May-emerging blue quills *(Paraleptophlebia mollis)*. This midseason blue quill appears on many of the trout streams we discuss in this book. On some of them this size-18 dark gray mayfly becomes an important hatch.

But you'll also find blue quills in July and August. If you visit the Middle Branch of the Genesee River in late July, you'll see the male spinners of the blue quill—the jenny spinner—undulating above fast-water sections. Martins Creek in southeastern Pennsylvania also holds a great late-summer blue quill hatch. You'll find this blue quill *(Paraleptophlebia guttata)* on many streams throughout Pennsylvania, New York, and New Jersey.

The late blue quill can take on especial importance if you encounter a chilly overcast or drizzly day in late summer. If you do—and if you know the stream you're fishing has this hatch—then get out early and prepare yourself for a fantastic morning of fly-fishing. I've enjoyed great angling more than once in July and August because I went fishing on one of those lousy days on a stream I knew held blue quills.

On New Jersey's South Branch of the Raritan River in mid-August I encountered two large mayfly hatches. The slate drake appeared in heavy numbers on the Ken Lockwood Gorge from 6 to 7:30 PM. The big Hex spinner *(Hexagenia atrocaudata)* appeared high over the water about 7:30 PM. This Hex hatch appears on many more streams than I once thought. Rich Keesler also found it on Martins Creek near Bangor, Pennsylvania.

Probably the most common hatches we found in the streams of Pennsylvania, New York, and New Jersey were the hendrickson, blue quill, sulphur, little blue-winged olive dun, and slate drake. By far the slate drake appears on more streams than any other mayfly in the three states.

SLATE DRAKE

George Slack uses a Light Cahill and an Adams almost exclusively on New Jersey's Pequest River throughout the summer. He finds both extremely effective patterns on that river. Why is the Adams so productive? It appropriately copies a slate drake.

You'll find slate drakes emerging from late May through much of June. They appear again in August and September. Yes, that's correct: Slate drakes have two generations per year. At one point anglers thought that they were seeing two or three separate slate drake species appearing in late spring and early summer; they thought a couple of other slate drake species emerged in fall. Entomologists now agree that much of this hatching activity—in the spring *and* the fall—can be attributed to one slate drake species: *Isonychia bicolor.*

You'll find some subtle differences in the two slate drake generations. I most often match the spring emerger with a size-12 imitation and the autumn slate drake with a size-14 pattern. You're probably aware that many of the nymphs crawl onto exposed rocks before they change into duns. Nymphs do this more often in the spring than they do in the fall.

I've fished the slate drake hatch for more than 30 years and have found that in some streams, nymphs often emerge in the surface film rather than on rocks. In off-color streams in particular—like those found in the Pocono region—slate drakes seem to emerge in the surface film.

Where slate drakes appear, they do so for more than 60 days out of the season. No wonder the Adams is such a productive pattern, especially throughout the summer! You'll find great slate drake hatches on McMichael, Tunkhannock, and Starrucca Creeks in northeastern Pennsylvania; on the South Branch of the Raritan in New Jersey; and on the East Branch of the Owego in New York.

HENDRICKSON

On almost every stream and river Bryan Meck, Craig Josephson, and I fly-fished, we saw or heard reports of a hendrickson hatch. Hendricksons vary in color and size from region to region—even from stream to stream.

On some streams and rivers you need a size-14 pattern to match the hatch. On the same stream later in the season and on other streams a size-16 pattern might be more appropriate. The reddish underbelly of the male dun seems to remain consistent from stream to stream.

Ask John Wettlaufer of Wind Gap, Pennsylvania, if New Jersey trout streams hold some good hendrickson hatches. He'll tell you about the time he fly-fished on Van Campen Brook in early April to avoid the heavy angling crowd on the Big Flat Brook. That afternoon John hit one of the best hendrickson hatches he's ever witnessed and he caught some good-sized streambred brown and native brook trout on an Adams pattern. Oatka Creek near Rochester, New York, also boasts great hendrickson hatches.

Most hendricksons appear from April 15 to April 30 in Pennsylvania and New Jersey. In New York you'll often see this species appearing the first week in May. The hatch usually lasts for about a week on any given stream.

LITTLE BLUE-WINGED OLIVE DUN

How I remember those great little blue-winged olive dun hatches on the San Juan in New Mexico! I fly-fished the area just below the Navajo Dam in late February a few years ago and hit a heavy hatch of these mayflies every afternoon for more than a week. But you don't have to travel that

The little blue-winged olive dun is found on many mid-Atlantic streams.

The sulphur is found on most of the overlooked streams.

far to see the hatch. It's extremely common on eastern waters. Whether I fly-fished on the South Branch of the Raritan, the Big Flat Brook, or the Rockaway River in New Jersey in September and October, I encountered little blue-winged olives.

I often call this and related species the "bad weather hatch." Add a little bit of rain, a drizzle, or just plain inclement weather in spring, late summer, or early fall and you'll likely see some of these small mayflies on the surface. Probably the best hatch of little blue-winged olives I ever hit occurred on central Pennsylvania's Fishing Creek. Bill Roberts of Chicago and I met on the stream on April 26 to fish and take photographs. The temperature that day never rose above 50 degrees and a cool drizzle fell the entire afternoon. Around 1 PM a spectacular hatch of blue quills appeared. Bill and I matched the hatch with a size-18 Blue Quill and had a modicum of success. About 2 PM the trout switched to a smaller mayfly that now appeared on the surface by the thousands. Because of the cold weather, few of these smaller mayflies took flight. Bill and I matched this second hatch with a size-20 Little Blue-Winged Olive Dun and caught some of Fishing Creek's most selective trout.

Be prepared to fish this hatch on almost every stream and river we've listed in this book. When you read the section on the South Branch of the

Raritan in New Jersey, you'll see how important this hatch can be—even in late summer.

SULPHUR

The word *sulphur* covers several hatches found on Pennsylvania, New York, and New Jersey streams. I usually limit the name to one of three hatches—*Ephemerella rotunda, E. invaria,* and *E. dorothea.* The *rotunda* sulphur usually appears first and is the largest of the three. On many limestone waters it's the most common of the three. Sometimes a size-14 Sulphur—but usually a size-16—matches this hatch. The *invaria* is next in size and usually appears from late May into late June. Often this second hatch can be matched with a size-16 pattern. The *dorothea* sulphur usually emerges the latest, from early June through much of July, and a size-18 will usually match the size. On some streams you'll find only one of the species; on others, two; and on some, all three of them.

If you have to choose only one time of the year to fish the streams and rivers we discuss in this book, you should select the latter part of May. Why? Most of these trout waters boast good—some even spectacular—hatches of sulphurs at that time. From Antietam Creek in south-central Pennsylvania to the South Branch of the Raritan River in New Jersey to Oatka Creek near Rochester, New York, you'll find great sulphur hatches in late May.

MARCH BROWN/GRAY FOX

Entomologists recently have clumped the March brown and gray fox together and classify both species as March browns. I still see some differences between them, however. The gray fox is usually smaller and lighter than the March brown. The gray fox also often appears in heavier numbers, and usually later in the day, than does the March brown. But I can't argue with skilled entomologists, so you'll note in the hatch charts for each stream we've lumped the two together, too.

NOTES ABOUT THE EMERGENCE CHART

The date of emergence listed in the chart is the average beginning day of the hatch for central Pennsylvania and northern New Jersey. Hatches will occur in the southern tier of New York about a week later than the dates listed. For example: You might easily see hendricksons on Oatka Creek near Rochester in early May rather than late April.

The "Duration" column should help you fish the hatches more readily. For years I've seen the whitefly on the Little Juniata River. Once the whitefly appears, it usually continues for 12 to 15 days. You'll see a 15 listed for the duration of this hatch. The brown drake is an extremely difficult hatch to fish. Why? It lasts for only a few days—in fact, the brown drake is possibly the mayfly with the shortest duration. If you do hit this hatch, you're in for some tremendous fly-fishing. You'll note a 5 under "Duration" for the brown drake, suggesting that the hatch appears for an average of 5 days on most streams.

What about patterns to match these hatches? You'll find many of the recipes to match common mayflies, caddisflies, and stoneflies listed in part 8.

Ken Rictor catches a trout during a quill gordon hatch on Wallace Run (see chapter 16).

EMERGENCE CHART

M = MAYFLY   C = CADDISFLY   S = STONEFLY

Scientific/common names	Emergence date (rough)	Time of day	Hook size	Duration (days)
Early black stonefly (S)	February and March	Noon–4 PM	14–18	30
Baetis tricaudatus (M)	April 1	10 AM–6 PM	18	50*
Dun: little blue-winged olive				
Spinner: rusty spinner				
Strophopteryx fasciata (S)	April 10	Afternoon	14	15
Early brown stonefly				
Paraleptophlebia adoptiva (M)	April 15	11 AM–4 PM	18	15
Dun: blue quill		Heaviest: 2–4		
Spinner: dark brown		Spinner: 4 PM		
Epeorus pleuralis (M)	April 18	1–3 PM	14	15
Dun: quill gordon		Spinner: 11:30 AM		
Spinner: red quill				
Ameletus ludens (M)	April 18	Afternoon	14	15
Dun: slate drake				
Spinner: quill gordon				
Chimarra atterima (C)	April 20	11 AM	16	15
Little black caddis				

M = MAYFLY   C = CADDISFLY   S = STONEFLY

Scientific/common names	Emergence date (rough)	Time of day	Hook size	Duration (days)
Ephemerella subvaria (M) Male dun: red quill Female dun: hendrickson Spinner: red quill	April 20	2–4 PM	14	7
Leptophlebia cupida (M) Dun: black quill Spinner: early brown	April 27	2–4 PM Spinner: 1–6 PM	14	10
Brachycentrus fuliginosus (C) Grannom	April 27	3–7 PM	14	7
Isoperla signata (S) Light stonefly	May 8	Afternoon	14	15
Ephemerella rotunda (M) Dun: sulphur dun Spinner: sulphur spinner	May 8	2–8 PM Spinner: 6–8 PM	16	30
Rhyacophilia lobifera (C) Green caddis	May 10	4–9 PM	14	15
*Baetis cinctutus*** (M) Dun: blue dun Spinner: rusty spinner	May 10	Afternoon	20	30

Ephemerella septentrionalis (M) Dun: pale evening Spinner: pale evening (3)***	May 18	8 PM	16	10
Leucrocuta aphrodite (M) Dun: pale evening Spinner: pale evening (2)	May 18	8 PM	16	30
Ephemerella invaria (M) Dun: sulphur dun Spinner: sulphur spinner	May 20	3–8 PM Spinner: 7 PM	16	30
Stenonema vicarium (M) Dun: American March brown Spinner: great red	May 20	10 AM–7 PM Spinner: 8 PM	12	20
*Stenonema fuscum***** (M) Dun: gray fox Spinner: ginger quill	May 15	Afternoon Spinner: 7–8 PM	14	20
Symphitopsyche slossanae (C) Spotted sedge	May 23	1–6 PM	14	15
Eurylophella bicolor (M) Dun: chocolate dun Spinner: chocolate spinner	May 25	Late morning, early afternoon	16	25
Stenonema ithaca (M) Dun: light cahill Spinner: light cahill	May 25	Evening	14	15

M = MAYFLY   C = CADDISFLY   S = STONEFLY

Scientific/common names	Emergence date (rough)	Time of day	Hook size	Duration (days)
Isonychia bicolor ***(M) Dun: slate drake Spinner: white-gloved howdy	May 25	Evening	12	60*
Epeorus vitreus (M) Male dun: light cahill Female dun: pink cahill Spinner: salmon spinner	May 25	Evening	14	20
Stenacron interpunctatum (M) Dun: light cahill Spinner: light cahill	May 25	Evening	14	30
Litobrancha recurvata (M) Dun: dark green drake Spinner: brown drake	May 25	1–8 PM Spinner: 7 PM	8	7
Ephemera simulans (M) Dun: brown drake Spinner: brown drake	May 25	8 PM	10	5
Ephemera guttulata (M) Dun: green drake Spinner: coffin fly	May 25	8 PM	8–10	7
Drunella cornuta (M) Dun: blue-winged olive Spinner: dark olive	May 26	Sporadic during day Dun: noon Spinner: 7–9 PM	14	14

Insect	Date	Time		
Serratella deficiens (M) Dun: dark blue quill Spinner: blue quill	May 26	Afternoon and evening	20	15
Ephemerella needhami (M) Dun: chocolate dun Spinner: chocolate spinner	May 30	Late morning, early afternoon Spinner: afternoon and evening	16	14
Pteronarcys dorsata (S) Giant stonefly	June 1	Evening	6	40
Ephemerella dorothea (M) Dun: sulphur dun Spinner: sulphur spinner	June 1	8 PM	18	45
Alloperla imbecilla (S) Little green stonefly	June 1	All day	16	45
Paraleptophlebia mollis (M) Dun: dark blue quill Male spinner: jenny spinner Female spinner: dark brown	June 3	10 AM–4 PM	18	30
Paraleptophlebia strigula (M) Dun: dark blue quill Male spinner: jenny spinner Female spinner: dark brown	June 5	Early morning–midafternoon	18	25
Psilotreta frontalis (C) Dark blue sedge	June 8	8 PM	14	15

M = MAYFLY   C = CADDISFLY   S = STONEFLY

Scientific/common names	Emergence date (rough)	Time of day	Hook size	Duration (days)
Drunella cornutella (M) Dun: blue-winged olive Spinner: dark olive	June 10	Dun: morning Spinner: evening	16	21
Dannella simplex (M) Dun: blue-winged olive Spinner: dark olive	June 15	Morning	20	10
Heptagenia marginalis (M) Dun: light cahill Spinner: olive cahill	June 15	8 PM	14	20
Stenonema pulchellum (M) Dun: cream cahill Spinner: cream cahill	June 15	Evening	14	30
Ephemera varia (M) Dun: yellow drake Spinner: yellow drake	June 15	Evening	10	40
Leucrocuta hebe (M) Dun: pale evening Spinner: pale evening	June 22	8 PM	16	40
Paraleptophlebia guttata (M) Dun: blue quill Male spinner: jenny spinner Female spinner: dark brown	June 25	Morning	18	75

Anthopotamanthus distinctus (M) Dun: golden drake Spinner: golden spinner	June 28	9 PM	12	15
Tricorythodes allectus (attratus) (M) Dun: pale olive Male spinner: dark brown Female spinner: reverse jenny	July 23	Morning	24	60
Ephoron leukon (M) Dun: white mayfly Spinner: white mayfly	August 15	7 PM	14	15
Hexagenia atrocaudata (M) Big slate drake Spinner: dark rusty	August 18	8 PM	8	10
Baetis tricaudatus (M) Dun: little blue Spinner: rusty spinner	September 1	Afternoon	20	50*
*Isonychia bicolor*** (M) Dun: slate drake Spinner: white-gloved howdy	September 10	Afternoon	14	60*
*Baetis cinctutus*** (M) Dun: blue dun Spinner: rusty spinner	September 10	Afternoon	20	30

*Includes both generations
**More than one generation per year
***Number of generations per year
****Now considered the same as the March brown

III.

Western Pennsylvania

You'll find some little-crowded, overlooked gems in western Pennsylvania. On many of these streams you'll see streambred trout—and, best of all, great hatches. Streams like Big Meadow Run in the southwestern corner of the state hold plenty of trout throughout the year; in late May you'll even see some green drakes on this water. One of the best small limestone streams in the state is Beaverdam Creek. We'll examine some of the best small and medium-sized streams in the area.

1. WOODCOCK CREEK

Rating: 4   DeLorme map: 29

Positives: *Some decent hatches around the end of May • Few fly-fishers*
Negatives: *Put-and-take fishing • Extremely low water in summer (especially above dam)*

Who ever heard of fly-fishing Woodcock Creek near Meadville? For weeks I looked for someone who was even faintly aware of this totally overlooked trout stream. Sure, plenty of bait-fishers travel here—just few fly-fishers. After several weeks of searching, I found Ken Haddix of Conneaut Lake, who unabashedly announced that he fly-fished on Woodcock Creek—at least for the first few weeks of the season. Ken operates a cooling and heating company out of Conneaut Lake in northwestern Pennsylvania, but if he had his preference, you'd find him on a trout stream almost every day of the week. He's fly-fished for a half-dozen years now, but he's well ahead of that in knowledge and skills.

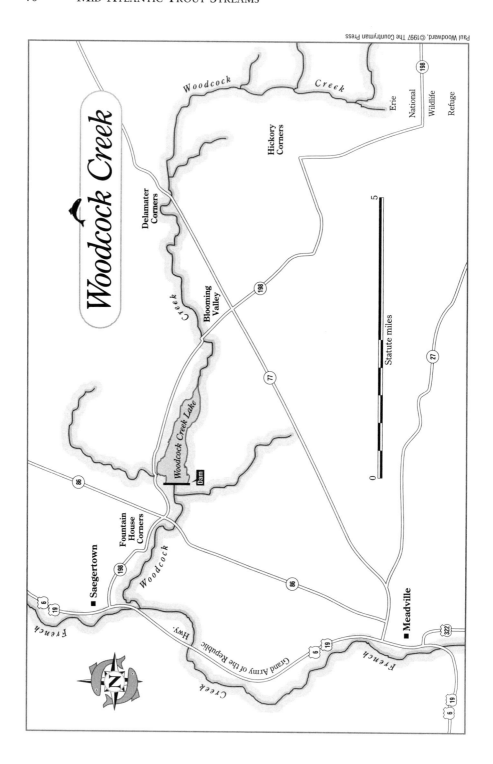

In late May, Ken and I headed to Woodcock Creek, located just off PA 86. Below Woodcock Creek Lake you'll find about a mile of productive trout water; there's easy access and parking below the dam. Here the stream meanders and forms some fairly deep pools and small, productive riffles. We looked at this lower end but decided to begin upstream, above the lake. In its upper area Woodcock becomes a small stream—averaging 15 to 30 feet wide in most places—with a few fairly deep pools. Ken and I fished on this upper end for at most a couple of hours and landed a half-dozen planted brown and rainbow trout.

But the best fly-fishing on Woodcock Creek usually occurs just below the dam. We headed downstream for the evening hatch. As we arrived on the water, dozens of cream cahills already took flight on this warm, late-spring evening. No trout rose to them, so Ken and I each continued to use a tandem rig made up of a Patriot dry fly and a Bead Head Pheasant Tail Nymph. The first couple of pools yielded nothing, and I thought we were in for a barren evening of fly-fishing. We continued upstream to within 500 yards of the bottom release. Ken caught the first trout on his wet fly— a heavy 15-inch rainbow. I caught the next one in the same small, productive riffle. Twenty minutes later we moved upstream from that riffle—but only after catching more than a half-dozen trout. We continued to pick up trout in just about every small pool we fished. That evening Woodcock Creek readily yielded its stocked trout. For the last hour, dozens of cream cahills took flight, but no trout fed on the rapidly escaping duns. Ken told me that on the previous evening, the trout had fed on duns. The duns had had more difficulty taking flight the evening before because of cooler air temperatures.

If you live in Ohio or in northwestern Pennsylvania, then Woodcock Creek is worth fishing. Because the release from the dam above is shallow, the lower end of the stream doesn't really experience the cooling effect a deeper lake would provide. Still, the stream does have some holdover trout and some cool water throughout the season. Ken Haddix took water temperatures for me and found the following:

June 14–August 3
Just below Woodcock Lake: 68–71 degrees
Above the dam at the bridge on PA 198: 67–72 degrees

Ken took the temperatures at 6 in the evening. When he recorded the temperatures in August, he saw several trout and a good hatch of little whiteflies, or *Caenis*. Try fishing the first mile below the dam in mid- to

Ken Haddix releases a trout caught on Woodcock Creek.

late May. You too should encounter plenty of cream cahills and rising trout at that time.

BEST TIMES TO FLY-FISH

April 15–May 15
Little blue-winged olive dun: afternoon, size 18
Blue quill: afternoon, size 18

May 15–June 15
March brown/gray fox: afternoon, size 12
Slate drake: evening, size 12
Cream cahill: evening, size 14
Sulphur: evening, size 16
Caenis: evening, size 26
Tan caddis: evening, size 14 or 16

June 16–August 31
Caenis: evening, size 26
Tan caddis: evening, size 14 or 16
Slate drake: evening, size 12

September 1–October 31
Little blue-winged olive dun: afternoon, size 18
Slate drake: afternoon, size 14

2. MARVIN CREEK

Delayed Harvest, Fly-Fishing Only—1.1 miles, from proximity of high voltage line (3 miles south of Smethport) downstream

Rating: 5   DeLorme map: 32

Positives: *Some good hatches • Easy access*
Negatives: *Warms somewhat in summer • Slow pools with few riffles in the delayed-harvest section*

Dave Kitchen moved from the Pittsburgh area to teach music at the high school in Smethport, Pennsylvania. He retired recently and now devotes much of his spare time to fly-fishing on Kettle, Potato, and Marvin Creeks. Dave lives on Potato Creek, so he sees that stream every day. But of the local streams, Dave prefers fly-fishing on Marvin Creek.

For several years I drove by this medium-sized stream just outside Smethport. US 6 parallels much of it. Each time I passed it on my way from Erie, I wondered if it held any good hatches or good numbers of trout. I finally was about to find out.

Dave and I fly-fished the delayed-harvest section in late May, a few days after he had seen some green drakes appear there. In this specially regulated water, you'll find almost too many stream improvement devices. Riffles in this section have been limited by log dams—too deep to fish anything but a heavily weighted Woolly Bugger. That day we almost gave up after an hour of barren fishing. Marvin Creek looked like a poor excuse for a trout stream after all.

But I wasn't ready to leave. Above the delayed-harvest area, we found a small meandering stream in no hurry to enter an impoundment below. Marvin Creek runs into Hamlin Dam in Smethport, just below the US 6 bridge. Dave Kitchen said that the locals call this the Tastee Freeze Bridge. He added that, in late May, you'll find dozens of trout feeding on midges and sulphurs in this stretch.

So the evening after that poor trip on the delayed-harvest area, I returned to Marvin Creek. I watched from the bridge at dusk and counted 30 rising trout. I hurriedly grabbed my gear from my car and waded into the stream just below the US 6 bridge. One trout after another took my Sulphur at the upper end of the dam. Talk about someone changing his opinion of a stream quickly—I certainly did! If you enjoy fishing over rising trout at dusk, you've got to try this area in May and early June.

You'll find other hatches on this 20- to 40-foot-wide freestone stream, too. If you fly-fish early in the season, you'll see blue quills and hendricksons on Marvin Creek. Look for parking pulloffs along US 6 in the delayed-harvest area.

Just below Hamlin Dam, Marvin Creek enters Potato Creek—but that's another chapter.

BEST TIMES TO FLY-FISH

April 1–May 1
Blue quill: afternoon, size 18
Hendrickson: afternoon, size 14
Black quill: afternoon, size 14

May 1–June 15
March brown/gray fox: afternoon, size 12
Sulphur: evening, size 16
Blue-winged olive dun: morning, size 14
Gray drake: afternoon and evening, size 12 or 14
Green drake: evening, size 10
Brown drake: evening, size 10
Slate drake: evening, size 12
Light cahill: evening, size 14

June 15–July 31
Yellow drake: evening, size 10
Slate drake: evening, size 12
Light cahill: evening, size 14

September 1–October 15
Slate drake: afternoon, size 14

3. POTATO CREEK

Rating: 5   DeLorme map: 33

*Positives: Some great hatches • Little fly-fishing pressure
Plenty of water • Some holdovers*
*Negatives: Some areas warm in summer • Some acid mine drainage
from tributaries on upper end of East Branch*

What fly shop has more than 1000 necks, a wide variety of fly-tying materials, thousands of unusual fly patterns for sale, and is located in a home? You'll find a setup like that in only one place—and I was fortunate enough to see it—Ron German's house on Banks Street in Smethport. If you're in

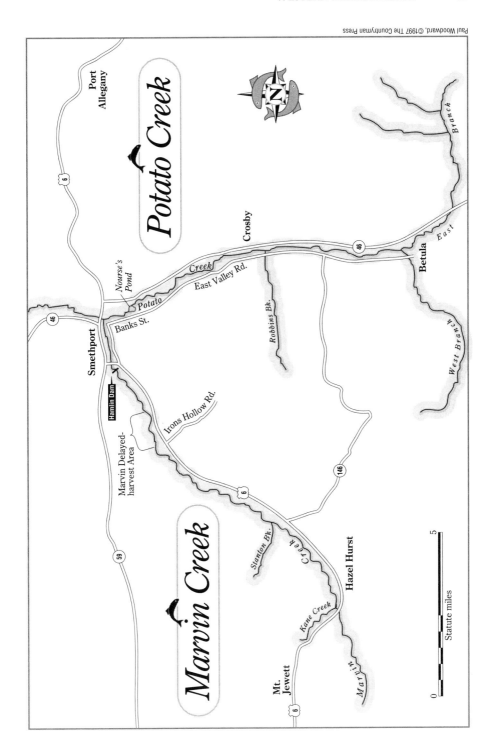

the area, you've got to stop by and meet this knowledgeable angler and see his unique store. It's the most complete fly-tying and fly-fishing shop within a 100-mile radius.

Ron German started tying flies when Roosevelt was in his second term as president of the United States—and he hasn't stopped. In fact he has his wife, Flossie, tying commercially for him. She ties great streamer patterns, including one I call the Pink Ughly.

Ron started fishing Potato and Marvin Creeks in 1922. He witnessed blizzardlike brown drake hatches and some good green drake hatches on these streams. He remembers the good old days when both the East and West Branches of Potato held excellent populations of wild trout. He bemoans the fact that the East Branch, although it does hold native brookies, has suffered from acid mine drainage. Railroad, Lyman, and Hamlin Runs add pollution to the upper end of the East Branch. Until the acid mine drainage abates in these tributaries, the upper end of the East Branch will remain relatively barren of any substantial native trout population.

Despite these problems, Ron still thinks Potato Creek holds some good fish. He feels that the lower end of the stream holds the best hatches, as well as a good trout population. He recommends fishing the area where Potato and Marvin join, right in the town of Smethport.

Dave Kitchen of Smethport joined me recently for a day of fly-fishing on Potato Creek. We hiked into an area known as Nourse's Pond. Here you'll find a 40- to 50-foot-wide stream with some heavy riffles and deep pools. Dave had been told that this area, too far from the road for normal stocking, had been float stocked. Not this year! Dave and I fly-fished this area for more than 2 hours. We didn't have a strike—didn't see a trout. We headed out of the area dejected. We did see a few green drakes, a couple of sulphurs, and some March browns emerge.

I suggested to Dave that we head to one of the bridges where planting had taken place. We ended up at a pool just below the bridge at Crosby. Within a few minutes, Dave caught the first trout here. By the time we ended our short excursion to this area, Dave and I had caught and released more than a dozen trout. Directly across the stream from us a bait-angler began fishing. I counted eight trout that he conked over the head with pliers—and still he kept fishing. Just think how great this stream would be if all anglers returned a few of their trout so everyone could have the opportunity to catch them.

We ended our long day on Potato just below Betula. Here I witnessed one of the heaviest gray drake spinner falls I've ever seen. At 7:30 in the evening, thousands of these large adults hovered above a long rapid.

You won't find many fly-fishers on Potato Creek at any time of the season. Jim Brown of Sharpsville is one of the few who regularly uses flies on this freestone stream. Jim's an exceptional fly-rod builder and fly-fisher. He usually spends the first week of the season on Potato and does well with nymphs.

But keep in mind that Potato Creek looks like a different stream in late summer. In late August I revisited the area I had fly-fished in May. The water level had dropped a foot. The West Branch might be a better choice later in the summer—it's 10 to 20 feet wide in its lower end, and its water runs cool all summer long.

PA 46 parallels much of the lower two-thirds of the stream. You'll find access to Potato Creek best in the middle section. There's parking at the bridge, and some pulloffs along PA 46. In total, there are about 10 miles of good fly-fishing on the main stem.

BEST TIMES TO FLY-FISH

April 15–May 15
Blue quill: afternoon, size 18
Hendrickson: afternoon, size 14
Quill gordon: afternoon, size 14
Black quill: afternoon, size 14
Grannom: afternoon, size 16
Cream caddis: afternoon and evening, size 14

Potato Creek, near Smethport, holds some great hatches.

May 16–June 15
Sulphur: evening, size 16
March brown/gray fox: afternoon, size 12
Gray drake: evening, size 12
Green drake: evening, size 12 (spotty)
Brown drake: evening, size 12
Slate drake: evening, size 12
Blue-winged olive dun: morning, size 14
Light cahill: evening, size 14

June 16–July 31
Slate drake: evening, size 12
Yellow drake: evening, size 10

August 1–October 15
Blue quill: morning, size 18
Slate drake: afternoon, size 14
Little blue-winged olive dun: afternoon, size 20

4. BENS CREEK

Rating: 5   DeLorme map: 73

Positives: *Native brook trout • Streambred brown trout • Good hatches*
Cold water all summer
Negatives: *Small brushy stream • Some acid mine drainage below*
Thomas Mills

"This stream holds cold water all summer long and has some great hatches throughout the season," Len Lichvar of Boswell boasted as he and Randy Buchanan of Richland Township pointed to recent stream improvements made by their Trout Unlimited (TU) chapter. "All we need in this stream now is to place some log dams and other devices to hold more fish."

"We had fifteen members of the Mountain Laurel Chapter of Trout Unlimited work yesterday on some stream devices so this stream can hold more trout," Randy added. He's president of the local TU organization, and they've spent many hours improving this small but productive trout stream.

Len, Randy, and I selected an area of Bens Creek just below the Casa Nova Restaurant to fly-fish. Some of the stream, especially the area just below PA 985 in Forwardstown, presents extremely tight fly-fishing. But downstream a few hundred yards the canopy opens, and you'll find casting on this 10- to 20-foot-wide stream fairly easy. Where we stood, Bens Creek was extremely small, so the three of us took turns at each productive-looking pool and riffle. While one man fished, the onlookers criticized his cast or the fact that he missed a trout. We fished a half-mile section of the stream where the chapter had already installed several stream improvement devices. The three of us hooked or missed maybe 20 trout, about half of them native brook trout and the other half streambred browns, in a leisurely 3-hour fishing trip. Not bad for the middle of the summer and the middle of a hot afternoon!

Bens Creek runs cold all summer long. We checked the temperature on that early-July midmorning and found a reading of 59 degrees. The heavy canopy over the stream helps.

You'll find good hatches in the upper section from above Forwardstown downstream a few miles. At Thomas Mills, several slugs of acid mine drainage enter. Although the Fish and Boat Commission stocks this lower end, fishing degenerates because of the slight discharges of acid. Hatches in the upper area include some green drakes and March browns in May and early June. As the season just gets under way you'll also find some blue quills, hendricksons, and quill gordons on Bens.

Len Lichvar and his group—known as the Stonycreek–Conemaugh River Improvement Project (SCRIP)—along with the Somerset County Conservation District and Lion Mining, have addressed the problem of acid mine drainage in the Thomas Mills area. The group has diverted effluent from the Rock Tunnel site into a series of holding ponds, which allow some of the iron to settle out before the effluent enters Bens Creek. This has helped the stream below with its trout and mayfly populations. The North Fork of Bens Creek enters the main stem near Johnstown. The Environmental Quality Board has recently upgraded the upper ends of the South and North Forks to exceptional value—a great designation for trout streams.

You'll find the most wild trout and holdovers in the upper end of Bens, above Thomas Mills. From there downstream you'll find a few wild trout, some hatches, and the best fishing early in the season. The North Fork joins the South Fork about 5 miles below Thomas Mills. PA 985 parallels much of the South Fork of Bens Creek before it enters the Stonycreek River near Johnstown. Look for parking at some of the bridges that cross Bens.

Next time you fly-fish on the South Fork or the main stem of Bens Creek, remember the work SCRIP and the Mountain Laurel Chapter of Trout Unlimited have done and continue to do to make Bens Creek a top-notch trout stream in Pennsylvania.

Randy Buchanan of the Mountain Laurel Chapter of Trout Unlimited points out some of the work his chapter has done on Bens Creek.

BEST TIMES TO FLY-FISH

April 10–May 10
Blue quill: afternoon, size 18
Quill gordon: afternoon, size 14
Little blue-winged olive dun: afternoon, size 20

May 11–June 15
Tan caddis: afternoon, size 14 or 16
March brown/gray fox: afternoon, size 12
Light cahill: evening, size 14
Green drake: evening, size 12
Slate drake: evening, size 12
Blue quill: morning, size 18
Giant stonefly: evening, size 6 (very spotty)
Sulphur: evening, size 16 or 18

June 16–August 31
Slate drake: evening, size 12
Blue quill: morning, size 18
Little yellow stonefly: afternoon, size 16
Little green stonefly: afternoon, size 16

Statute miles

Claysburg

Sproul

Boiling Spring Run

SR 3005

SR 4019

SR 4031

Conrail

220

Beaverdam Creek

164

56

Beaverdam Creek

N

Conemaugh

53

River

219

160

56

Little

219

56

Johnstown

Stonycreek

Bens Creek

403

Mill Creek Pike

River

Somerset Pike

Creek

985

Thomas
Mills

271

N. Fork

Quemahoning
Reservoir

S. Fork

Bens

Forwardstown

985

30

219

5. BEAVERDAM CREEK

Rating: 7   DeLorme map: 74

Positives: *Cold limestone stream • Good hatches • Streambred brown
trout • Plenty of deep pools*
Negatives: *Relatively short • Small and brushy stream*

Before you read about this overlooked but extremely productive stream,
you've got to promise not to keep one of these trout. If you kill trout, even
only occasionally, then I don't want you fly-fishing on this limestone stream.
If you promise not to keep one trout caught here, then you can continue
reading about this small but excellent trout water—Beaverdam Creek, near
Claysburg.

As with so many neglected streams, I had never fly-fished Beaverdam
Creek until this past year, in preparation for this book. For the past 3
years I had traveled along the stream on my way to Bob's Creek in southwestern Pennsylvania. Not until I tried Beaverdam for the first time did I
realize the quality of fly-fishing that this small 10- to 20-foot-wide stream
had to offer.

I invited Bob Budd of nearby Hollidaysburg to join me on the stream
one late-July evening. During the day, Bob's a skilled eye surgeon—but
give him a day or an evening off and he becomes one of the most expert
fly-fishers I've had the privilege of knowing. He began fly-fishing at a young
age—he's been using artificials for the past 25 years. Any and every chance
he gets, Bob casts on area streams.

As we collected our gear at streamside, Bob and I talked with an angler
who had just quit for the day. This bait-fisher claimed Beaverdam as his
home stream. Just a couple of years ago, he said, he'd caught a couple of
brown trout more than 20 inches long. When I asked the old-timer if
Beaverdam Creek had any streambred browns, he said no.

Bob and I walked downstream a half mile and fished back up toward the
cars. Bob used a tandem with a size-12 Patriot dry fly and a size-16 Bead
Head Pheasant Tail Nymph. In the next hour he caught and released seven
trout—six streambred and one stocked trout. A heavy, sudden midsummer
thunderstorm chased the two of us back to our cars. When I repeated what
the old-timer had said about streambred trout in Beaverdam Creek, Bob
and I just looked at each other and grinned. Despite the old-timer's words,
Beaverdam truly holds a good supply of wild brown trout.

On another occasion, I fly-fished Beaverdam Creek on a hot July afternoon for about an hour. I first checked the water temperature and recorded
a reading of 64 degrees—not bad on a mid-80-degree day in mid-July. It's

difficult to reach the stream, and there are only a few access areas. I parked my car and hiked down the old railroad track a half mile to the point where the stream abuts the tracks. Here I began fly-fishing in very close quarters. Willows, bushes, and high weeds on almost every cast seemed to reach out to grab my tandem, also made up of a Patriot and Bead Head. Still, in a 100-yard stretch of water I picked up four streambred brown trout. Two of these trout measured more than a foot long, and remember, this was a hot July day.

In some areas of the stream, although they're not marked, fishing is not allowed. The limestone quarry area at Queen is off limits, as are some other areas. If you plan to fly-fish, try the section downstream from State Route (SR) 3005. Here there's a good mile of water before the stream becomes the Frankstown Branch of the Juniata River. You can reach the stream just off US 220 at the Sproul exit. There's parking at the SR 3005 bridge.

If you like to fish when hatches appear, then the best time to hit Beaverdam Creek is near the end of May. You'll see plenty of sulphurs emerging and a good number of streambred and stocked trout rising. But Beaverdam Creek can also come alive with rising trout late in the season with its own trico hatch. Spend any morning in late July, August, or September and you'll see good trico hatches in areas of the stream where there's little canopy.

Remember, you've promised to return these trout!

BEST TIMES TO FLY-FISH

April 10–May 10
Little blue-winged olive dun: afternoon, size 20
Blue quill: afternoon, size 18

May 11–June 15
Sulphur: evening, size 16
Gray fox: afternoon, size 14
Blue quill: morning, size 18
Blue-winged olive dun: morning, size 14

June 16–July 30
Blue quill: morning, size 18
Yellow drake: evening, size 12
Sulphur: evening, size 18
Trico: morning, size 24

August 1–September 30
Trico: morning, size 24
Blue quill: morning, size 18
Little blue-winged olive dun: afternoon, size 20

6. DUNBAR CREEK

Fly-Fishing Only—4.1 miles, from the confluence of Glade Run and
Dunbar Creek downstream to the stone quarry along SR 1055

Rating: 5   DeLorme map: 86

Positives: Good cold water • Beautiful setting • Plenty of water to fly-fish
Negatives: Some acid mine drainage • Sparse hatches • Some poaching

"Homer, come downstream," bellowed Ron Dorula, owner of the Fur "N" Feather fly shop in Uniontown. Ron ties some of the best midge patterns I've ever seen in my more than 40 years of angling; he's a great fly-fisher, too, and he and some of his friends accompanied us for a day of fly-fishing on Dunbar Creek.

I added: "We got 'em cornered."

Ron wanted Homer Wehe to wade downstream to fish a deep, 30-foot-long pool where he had just spotted a half-dozen brook trout. Homer obliged and waded down to the deep pool. Now five of us were in the pool in Dunbar's delayed-harvest section. We picked up a couple of trout in this slower section and quit for the day. We had already spent 6 successful hours on the stream and caught more than 20 trout.

Before we headed back to the car, Ron Dorula, Mark DeFrank, and Eugene Gordon seined a section of the stream looking for nymphs. Eugene showed me a green drake and said that this large mayfly appears in heavy enough numbers in late May and early June to bring Dunbar's trout to the surface.

You won't find too many mayflies in any heavy numbers here, though. Acid mine drainage from a tributary, Glade Run, affects Dunbar Creek below. Eugene Gordon said that he has recorded pH levels from 6.3 to 6.7. Scientists use this as a measure of acidity; 7.0 is neutral. Any number lower than that suggests some acidity. If authorities made a concerted effort to elevate the pH on Glade Run, it would have a beneficial effect on the insect population of Dunbar Creek. In the future, they do plan to add some limestone to the tributary. Ron Dorula, Eugene Gordon, and Mark DeFrank feel confident that this experiment will succeed.

Eugene Gordon releases a trout caught on Dunbar Creek.

Despite the acidity, Dunbar Creek still holds some hatches—few of them fishable, however. Eugene Gordon, an excellent fly-fisher and mayfly collector, has studied the hatches on Dunbar extensively. He can also recall comments from many anglers in years past about the hatches they saw on the stream. Some told Eugene about the heavy quill gordon hatch that Dunbar Creek held at one time. Hatches aren't as heavy now as they were then, but you can still find some March browns and sulphurs in late May. Eugene has fished over trout rising to green drakes on several occasions. Ask him about the good stonefly hatches on the Dunbar, too, especially the olive stonefly that appears in July and August. Eugene and Mark have even seen a few tricos on Dunbar this past year.

But because the mayfly hatches are often sparse, what do you use on Dunbar Creek? Ron Dorula always carries an ample supply of midge patterns. He sees them on the stream on almost every trip. Dunbar also holds some good caddisfly and cranefly hatches.

What advantages does a stream like Dunbar have? First, there's plenty of open water to fly-fish. Dunbar flows mainly through state game lands, and you don't have to worry about private property. Second, it rests in a picturesque, idyllic valley with plenty of huge boulders, a heavy canopy of trees, and rhododendrons along the streambank. The 20- to 30-foot-wide stream drops quickly and has plenty of rapids and boulder-strewn pools. The state has designated 4.1 miles of delayed-harvest, fly-fishing-only water on the middle part.

The Chestnut Ridge Chapter of Trout Unlimited and the Dunbar Sportsmen have spent hours cleaning up debris along the stream and jointly sponsor a fishing derby for youngsters. Now that the local TU organization has evolved, Dunbar Creek has a chance of growing into a much better trout stream. With its help, Dunbar Creek might just become one of the better streams in southwestern Pennsylvania.

But Dunbar Creek also has some serious problems. I mentioned earlier that acid mine drainage has hurt the mayfly hatches on the stream. Poaching on the stream is apparent as well. Some anglers don't seem to know or care about the special regulations on the delayed-harvest section of Dunbar Creek.

What about the quality of fishing on the stream? You'll find brook trout and some browns in the upper end of the fly stretch. You'll also catch some native brook trout. Does Dunbar hold any large trout? Eugene Gordon remembers the day he caught a hefty brown trout on a fly several years ago. Ron Dorula landed a heavy brook trout about 20 inches long several years ago, and Mark DeFrank landed a 17-inch brookie.

You can reach the stream off US 119 between Connellsville and

Uniontown. Follow the signs to the town of Dunbar. SR 1055 parallels the lower end of the stream, and Township Road (TR) 782 the middle part. Above the fly stretch you'll find little access to the stream, although several dirt roads cross this upper part around Jumonville. You can get additional information on stream conditions and hatches from Ron Dorula, Mark DeFrank, or Eugene Gordon at Fur "N" Feather.

Ask Ron or Eugene what is one of the best trout streams in southwestern Pennsylvania. They'll proudly tell you about Dunbar Creek and some of the work their local TU chapter has done.

BEST TIMES TO FLY-FISH

March 25–April 30
Little black stonefly: afternoon, size 14 or 16
Black caddis: afternoon, size 18
Gray caddis: afternoon, size 16
Blue quill: afternoon, size 18 (spotty)
Quill gordon: afternoon, size 14 (spotty)

May 1–May 31
Sulphur: evening, size 16
Gray fox : afternoon, size 12
Tan caddis: afternoon and evening, size 14
Little yellow stonefly: evening, size 16
Brown stonefly: evening, size 14
Green drake: evening, size 10 or 12

June 1–June 30
Green drake: evening, size 10 or 12
Light cahill: evening, size 14
Sulphur: evening, size 16
Brown stonefly: evening, size 14
Orange cranefly: afternoon, size 10 or 12
Little yellow stonefly: evening, size 16

July 1–July 31
Brown stonefly: evening, size 14
Light cahill: evening, size 14
Olive stonefly: evening, size 18
Little yellow stonefly: evening, size 18

August 1–September 30
Olive stonefly: evening, size 18
Light cahill: evening, size 14

Trico: morning, size 24 (spotty)
Note: Black midges in sizes 20–24 are prevalent throughout the season.

7. BIG MEADOW RUN

Rating: 5   DeLorme map: 86

Positives: *Some good hatches • Reminiscent of a great north-central Pennsylvania stream*
Negatives: *Few productive pools • Some acid mine drainage in the lower end • Only a small section of the stream open to public fishing*

Look at this stream just above the Ohiopyle State Park and you'd swear you're fly-fishing on a Potter County freestone stream. But you're not—you're fishing one of the top trout streams in southwestern Pennsylvania—Big Meadow Run.

I recently had an opportunity to fly-fish this 30-foot-wide, quality freestone stream for a second time with Paul Miller, originally from nearby Mill Run. Paul knows the stream well and fishes it expertly. As Paul and I reached the upper area of the open water, he reminisced about the stream. "See that abandoned ball field just across the road—we used to play a group from Ohiopyle. We'd play them for a keg of beer. Little did I think I'd be fly-fishing on this stream 20 years later."

Paul, Craig Cheselke, and I selected the stretch across from the old ball field to begin fishing. As the three of us waded into the stream, a few blue-winged olives emerged from the riffle on the far shore. I headed downstream and Paul fished near the Community Church. As I waded along, I noticed a dimple in the water near the far shore. I cast a size-12 Patriot over the disturbance and a heavy fish immediately hit the pattern. I landed a healthy 12-inch brown trout. A few casts later, a rainbow hit the same pattern in midstream.

Meanwhile, just 100 feet upstream, Paul Miller saw a trout rise. He cast a caddis pattern just above the rise, the trout struck, and he missed it. Craig and I kidded him, saying that he had lost his opportunity to catch a trout. Paul didn't quit. He continued to cast in the same general area. On about the 10th cast, another trout hit the caddis, and this time Paul didn't miss.

After a noontime break, the three of us headed downstream to fly-fish nearer the Youghiogheny River. Here Big Meadow ranges from 20 to 40 feet wide, with a few deep pools and productive riffles. Here also the state has proposed to place a delayed-harvest area. Craig Cheselke said the

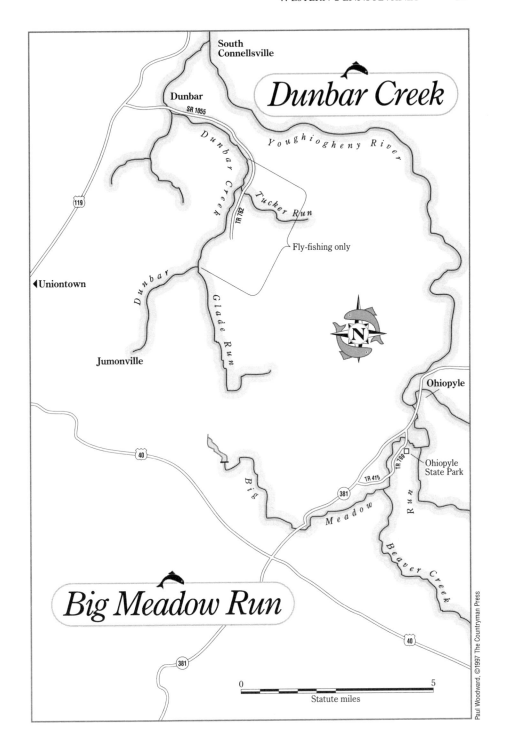

South
Connellsville

Dunbar

SR 1055

Dunbar Creek

Dunbar Creek

Youghiogheny River

119

TR 782

Tucker Run

Fly-fishing only

Uniontown

Dunbar

Glade Run

Jumonville

Ohiopyle

40

TR 415

TR 788

Ohiopyle
State Park

381

Big

Meadow

Run

Beaver Creek

Big Meadow Run

40

381

0   5

Statute miles

Paul Woodward, ©1997 The Countryman Press

Chestnut Ridge Chapter of Trout Unlimited and Ohiopyle State Park have cooperated totally to bring this much-needed project to fruition. The chapter plans to make some stream improvements on this section as well. With just a few stream improvement devices in place, this section will hold many more trout than it now does. If the delayed-harvest section comes to fulfillment, look for some great fly-fishing in the state park.

Still, I've only rated Big Meadow Run a 5, and that's due to several problems. First, there are only about 3 or 4 miles of productive water. You'll find it from Beaver Creek downstream on the main stem. Just a few years ago, the state planted trout in Big Meadow upstream almost to US 40. Now much of that area is posted and no longer stocked. Also, in Big Meadow's lower end, before it enters the Youghiogheny River, some acid mine drainage from Laurel Run enters. This degenerates the quality of the water below.

By the way, one of Meadow's tributaries, Beaver Creek, has some excellent club water on it. If you get the opportunity to fish this private section, do it. Recently I fly-fished this tributary, again with Paul Miller, for an afternoon, and I was amazed by the quality of the angling and the number of trout. Daryl Bassett, stream manager of the Beaver Creek Anglers, showed me some vials he had of this stream's hatches. There were green drakes, slate drakes, light cahills, and pink ladies. As Paul and I fly-fished the stream, we noted some green drakes emerging that early-June evening.

Big Meadow Run itself boasts a good number of hatches, including the green drake. Along with Beaver Creek, it has some March browns in late May. In early June you'll find some blue-winged olives and slate drakes, along with downwings like little yellow stoneflies and little green stoneflies.

Big Meadow Run holds a good supply of holdover trout. In fact, after watching a recent electrofishing episode by the Pennsylvania Fish and Boat Commission, Eugene Gordon, a local fly-fishing expert, believes there might even be some streambred rainbows in the stream.

If you're in the Ohiopyle area in southwestern Pennsylvania, especially after Memorial Day, it's worthwhile fishing this freestone stream for a day. Why after Memorial Day? You'll probably see few, if any, anglers along the stream after that holiday. You can access the stream off PA 381 at Ohiopyle. Meadow Run Road (TR 799) gets you to the section just below Beaver Creek. You'll find plenty of parking near the Community Church and downstream in the state park. Big Meadow Run ends its 6-mile journey, emptying into the Youghiogheny River just outside Ohiopyle.

BEST TIMES TO FLY-FISH

April 15–May 10
Blue quill: afternoon, size 18
Quill gordon: afternoon, size 14
Little blue-winged olive dun: afternoon, size 18

May 11–June 15
March brown/gray fox: afternoon, size 12
Sulphur: evening, size 16
Slate drake: evening, size 12
Green drake: evening, size 12
Blue-winged olive dun: afternoon, size 16
Light cahill: evening, size 14
Pink lady: evening, size 14

June 16–July 31
Slate drake: evening, size 12
Blue-winged olive dun: afternoon, size 16
Little yellow stonefly: afternoon and evening, size 18
Little green stonefly: afternoon and evening, size 18

September 1–October 15
Slate drake: afternoon, size 14
Little blue-winged olive dun: afternoon, size 20

IV.

Central Pennsylvania

Central Pennsylvania contains some of the best trout fishing in the eastern United States. Who hasn't heard of such great waters as Penns Creek, Fishing Creek, and Spring Creek? But, as I said in the introduction, in the past few years these and other well-known streams have suffered from a lot of angling pressure. Why not avoid these crowded waters, especially from April through early May, and opt for one of the lesser-known streams discussed in this chapter? Why not try streams like Rock Run, Pleasant Stream, and Wallace Run? Better yet, try the Tioga River above Blossburg or Baker Run a few miles north of Lock Haven. You'll probably be the only fly-fisher on the entire stream. Scout around and you'll find a variety of overlooked streams in central Pennsylvania. We discuss only a few of them here.

8. GENESEE RIVER

Rating: 6   DeLorme map: 34

Positives: *Some good hatches • Native and streambred trout*
Negatives: *The three branches are small and lined with alders at spots*

I drove down Potter County's Ulysses Township Road (TR) 410 to where it intersects with TR 408, stopped, got out of the car, and just stared. I looked to the east and south and saw a tributary just a couple of hundred yards away that flowed into the famous Pine Creek. I gazed off to the west and less than a quarter mile away saw a trickle of water that flowed into the upper end of the Allegheny River. Then I glanced to the north, a few hundred feet down a rolling hill, and caught a glimpse of a small brook that would become the Middle Branch of the Genesee River. Not bad—looking east and seeing a stream that eventually flowed into the Atlantic Ocean—west and seeing the water that someday would enter the Gulf of Mexico—and north to watch part of a river that emptied into one of the Great Lakes—and they all began within a few hundred yards of where I stood.

Then I headed north to check out the main stem and the Middle and West Branches of the Genesee River. The Genesee is one of those unusual rivers that flows north, into Lake Ontario at Rochester. On its way, especially near Wellsville, New York, it becomes a relatively good trout stream. (See Craig Josephson's discussion of that river on page 150.) But few anglers fly-fish the three branches of the river in Pennsylvania. Why not? There are only a couple of miles of big water (30 to 50 feet wide) in Pennsylvania before the river enters New York State. So what you're fishing in the Keystone State is three separate but very similar small streams with cold water, good hatches, and few other anglers. The two branches and the main stem all range from 10 to 20 feet wide and present some definite casting problems for even the most skilled fly-fisher. All three contain overgrown willow and alder banks, swamps, and plenty of beaver dams. And on all three you'll find a good number of cool springs entering throughout that add shots of cold water to the branches. All three flow 6 to 10 miles through a mixture of farmland, woodland, and swampland before they join near the town of Genesee.

I recently met Chuck and Mary Downing in the small, friendly town of Genesee. The main stem of the Genesee River flows just a couple of hundred feet from Chuck's house. On his property Chuck has a cool spring entering the main stem. Look in a small pond where that spring enters and you'll see plenty of brook trout. (Chuck and Mary allow fishing on their property, but they appreciate it when anglers ask permission.)

Chuck and other locals think that the West Branch of the Genesee is the best of the lot. Surveys by the Pennsylvania Fish and Boat Commission seem to bear this out. Biologists found a good number of trout on this branch—many of them wild fish. Chuck took me up the West Branch for an evening of fly-fishing. In less than 2 hours on the West Branch, I caught 10 trout. Not bad for a late-July evening and low-water conditions! All three branches hold native brookies, streambred browns, and planted trout.

I prefer fishing the West Branch, especially the section several miles upstream of the town of Genesee near a small town called Chapmans. Here you'll find some deep pools and productive riffles and plenty of wild trout. You'll also find difficult casting, so bring a 7- or 8-foot fly-rod with

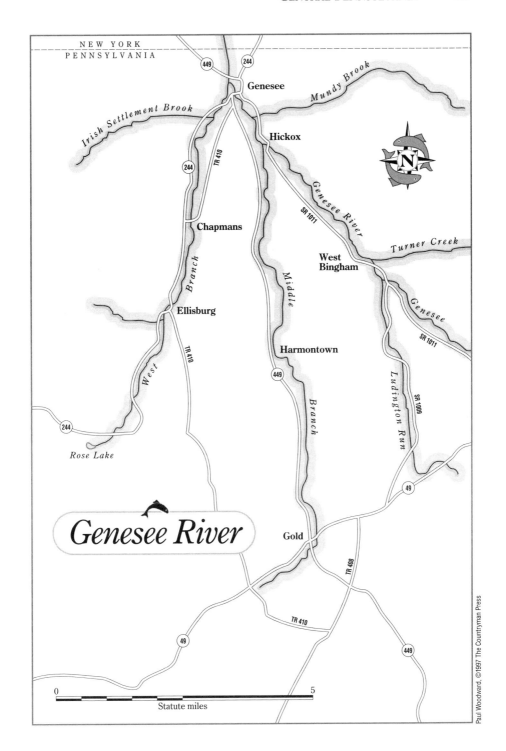

NEW YORK
PENNSYLVANIA

449 244

Genesee

Mundy Brook

Hickox

Irish Settlement Brook

244

TR 410

Genesee River

SR 1011

N

Chapmans

Turner Creek

West
Bingham

Branch

Genesee

Ellisburg

SR 1011

TR 410

Harmontown

West

449

SR 1009

Ludington Run

244

Middle

Branch

Rose Lake

49

Genesee River

Gold

TR 408

49

TR 410

449

0   5

Statute miles

Paul Woodward, ©1997 The Countryman Press

you. The West Branch begins only a few miles east of Oswayo Creek, one of my top freestone streams in the state.

One of the few anglers who does fly-fish the Genesee River and its branches in Pennsylvania is Bill Fries of Salamanca, New York. Bill has seen mayflies on the surface, especially in early and midseason. He's fished over hatches of sulphurs on the stream for more than a decade.

Will you find any large trout in the river? Just visit the Mini-Mart in Hickox, where the Middle Branch joins the main stem. Inside you'll see two large rainbow trout, both more than 20 inches long, mounted on the wall. The Genesee truly holds some big fish. From Hickox downriver the Genesee grows larger. Just a short distance below, in the town of Genesee, the West Branch enters. When all three join you'll find a large stream— but it flows north into New York just a mile or two later.

You can access the main stem from State Route (SR) 1009 and SR 1011. PA 449 parallels the Middle Branch, and PA 244 the West Branch. PA 244 is a rough, narrow, blacktop road. You'll find numerous pulloffs along all three branches.

BEST TIMES TO FLY-FISH

April 10–May 15
Little blue-winged olive dun: afternoon, size 20
Blue quill: afternoon, size 18
Hendrickson: afternoon, size 14
Grannom: afternoon, size 16

May 15–June 15
Sulphur: evening, size 16 or 18
March brown/gray fox: afternoon, size 12
Light cahill: evening, size 14
Light stonefly: afternoon, size 14
Slate drake: evening, size 12
Green drake: evening, size 10 (spotty)

June 16–July 31
Blue quill: morning, size 18
Trico: morning, size 24 (spotty)
Yellow drake: evening, size 12
Light cahill: evening, size 14
Golden drake: evening, size 14
Tan caddis: evening, size 16
Little yellow stonefly: afternoon and evening, size 16
Little green stonefly: afternoon and evening, size 16

August 1–September 30
Blue quill: morning, size 18
Slate drake: afternoon, size 14
Trico: morning, size 24

9. TIOGA RIVER

Rating: 6   DeLorme map: 36

*Positives: Cold water all summer • Plenty of native brook trout
Good pocket water
Negatives: Some acid mine drainage in several tributaries*

At the age of 7, he caught his first trout on the Tioga River. He still remembers that strike back in 1923. To this day he can see the 8-inch brook trout that came up from the bottom of a 3-foot-deep pool to grab his Royal Coachman dry fly. That changed this angler's point of view forever and made an indelible mark on his young mind. Charlie Pierce of nearby Blossburg cheerfully recalls his first fishing trip with a fly-rod on the Tioga River. He still fly-fishes on the river more than seven decades later.

That first success with the dry fly really influenced Charlie for the rest of his life. He has tied flies commercially in the past and has taught fly-tying classes to hundreds of enthusiasts in north-central Pennsylvania. Today, with eight decades behind him, Charlie still ties fantastic flies and casts a fly-rod like a true expert.

Talk about overlooked streams—the Tioga River makes the top of the list. How can this happen to such a beautiful stream? Look closely at the river in Blossburg. Here the Tioga looks like dozens of others affected severely by acid mine drainage. Here you'll find exposed rocks coated with telltale red stains. And, most important, here you'll find no insect life or trout. Most people traveling over this creek along busy US 15 don't realize that just a few miles upriver, above Fall Brook, the Tioga River becomes an exceptional trout stream—one filled with plenty of fair-sized native brook trout and some hatches.

Recently, in mid-July, Charlie Pierce and I fly-fished this spectacular 20- to 30-foot-wide river at the County Bridge State Park section. No hatch was occurring at that time, so I showed Charlie how the tandem works. I used a Patriot dry fly and a size-16 Bead Head Pheasant Tail Nymph. In not much more than an hour of fly-fishing, Charlie and I landed or hooked a dozen trout in the river. Not bad for the middle of a hot July afternoon!

The river gets a lot of angling pressure in the state park area, especially early in the season, but few fly-fishers. In fact, another fly-fisher, Jamie Sheridan of Troy, appeared on the water the afternoon Charlie and I were there. He was so startled to see other fly-fishers that he came upstream several hundred yards just to greet us and talk. Jamie spends a couple of days a week fly-fishing on the river and rarely, if ever, sees anyone else doing so. He prefers the section just below the state park. Here he catches plenty of native brook trout.

The Tioga has some problems, chief of which is the acid mine drainage that enters the main stem. The upper 8 miles of the river run fairly pure, though, with little shots of acid coming in from Fellows Creek and Rundall Run. The state has recently begun liming the lower end just above Blossburg, and it's hoped that within a decade or two trout will show up in this area again. The Hillside Rod and Gun Club raises and stocks trout for the Tioga River.

You can also reach the river from the south by taking PA 414 to Gleason, then turning north on SR 2021. Access the upper end of the river off a dirt road, SR 2014. You'll find the best fly-fishing from the headwaters downriver to Fall Brook. That's about 7 miles of good trout fishing. The section from Fall Brook upriver to the state park seems to have little pressure during much of the season. The camping area at the state park does, however, get a lot of angling pressure all summer long. Just above the campsite you'll find some deep water and native brook trout. There's plenty of parking in this state park area.

The Tioga River holds good hatches, including some green drakes, slate drakes, and blue-winged olives—all found in late May and early June. The stream also holds some good caddis hatches in May, especially tan caddis.

Next time you go through Blossburg on US 15, remember Charlie Pierce and his more than 70 years of fishing on the Tioga River. Remember, too, not to judge this river by what it looks like in town. Travel upriver several miles to see the true Tioga and its native trout.

BEST TIMES TO FLY-FISH

April 10–May 10
Little blue-winged olive dun: afternoon, size 20
Blue quill: afternoon, size 18
Quill gordon: afternoon, size 18
Hendrickson: afternoon, size 14

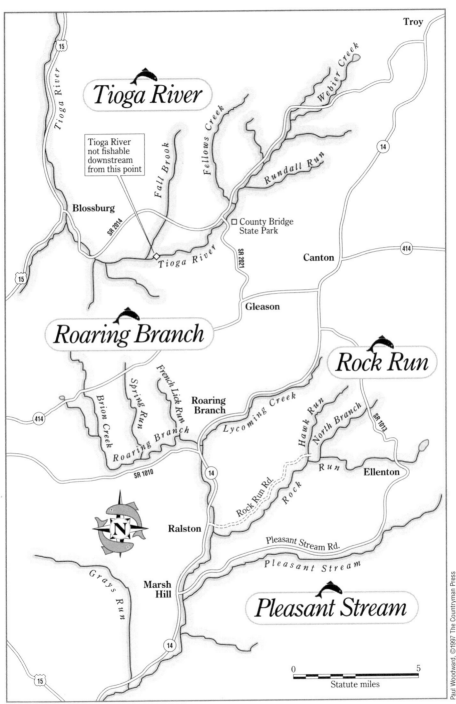

Tioga River

Tioga River
not fishable
downstream
from this point

Blossburg

County Bridge
State Park

Canton

Tioga River

Gleason

Roaring Branch

Rock Run

Roaring
Branch

Ralston

Marsh
Hill

Pleasant Stream Rd.

Pleasant Stream

Pleasant Stream

0   5
Statute miles

Paul Woodward, ©1997 The Countryman Press

Charlie Pierce of Blossburg wades into position to fish
for rising trout on the Tioga River.

May 11–June 30

Light stonefly: afternoon, size 14
Sulphur: evening, size 16
March brown/gray fox: afternoon, size 12
Green drake: evening, size 10 (spotty)
Slate drake: evening, size 12
Blue quill: morning, size 18
Tan caddis: afternoon and evening, size 14 or 16
Little yellow stonefly: afternoon and evening, size 16

July 1–August 31

Slate drake: evening, size 14
Dark gray caddis: morning, size 18

September 1–October 15

Slate drake: afternoon, size 14
Little blue-winged olive dun: afternoon, size 20

10. ROARING BRANCH

Rating: 6   DeLorme map: 36

Positives: *Spectacular stream • Spectacular setting*
Some good hatches
Negatives: *Difficult access • Difficult to wade once on the stream*

Although Rock Run (see page 73) may be the most spectacular stream in Pennsylvania, Roaring Branch has got to be second in line. It boasts some of the most picturesque pools of any stream I've ever seen in the state—for that matter, on any stream in the United States. But access to the stream is difficult, and even once you're there, you'll find wading treacherous.

Roaring Branch is not for the faint of heart. I recently fly-fished a section 2 miles upstream from its juncture with Lycoming Creek. I parked the car at the top of a steep hill and hiked down a trail leading to the stream. Once on the stream, I headed up a narrow, steep valley. I fished for a couple of hundred feet before I was confronted with a huge, 10-foot-deep pool. A boulder occupied the right side of the stream; on the left I was confronted with a sheer cliff. I had to walk back downstream to the trail and hike back up to the car.

Roaring Branch holds some hefty trout, however. Why? Look at the size, depth, and hiding spots in some of the pools and you'll know instantly that the trout have plenty of protection. Add to these advantages a wide variety of food, and you too will have to believe people like Russell Machmer of nearby Canton, who verifies reports of 4- to 6-pound trout caught annually on Roaring Branch.

What about hatches? Roaring Branch holds some good ones. You'll find some nice blue quill hatches on the stream, along with a fair green drake hatch. As with the other nearby freestones, you'll also find a good quantity of light cahills.

How do you reach this unique stream? Roaring Branch flows into Lycoming Creek just south of the town with the same name. You can reach the upper part of the stream off PA 14 on SR 1010. Look for pulloffs along SR 1010. You'll have to hike about a half mile down to the water. You'll agree once you've seen this gem that it's one of the most spectacular streams in the state.

In fact, take an entire day and fish the three tributaries to Lycoming Creek: Roaring Branch, Rock Run, and Pleasant Stream (see below) are all worth the time.

Note the huge rocks on the Roaring Branch.

BEST TIMES TO FLY-FISH

April 10–May 10
Blue quill: afternoon, size 18
Quill gordon: afternoon, size 14
Early brown stonefly: afternoon, size 14
Hendrickson: afternoon, size 14

May 11–June 30
Light stonefly: afternoon, size 14
Sulphur: evening, size 16 or 18
March brown/gray fox: afternoon, size 12
Tan caddis: evening, size 14
Light cahill: evening, size 14
Blue quill: morning, size 18
Green drake: evening, size 12 (spotty)
Slate drake: evening, size 12
Little yellow stonefly: evening, size 18
Little green stonefly: evening, size 18

11. ROCK RUN

Rating: 6   DeLorme map: 36

Positives: *Spectacular scenery • Spectacular stream*
Holdover and native trout
Negatives: *Watch your step • Difficult access*

What stream in Pennsylvania has spectacular ledge-lined deep pools and is considered by those who fish it regularly the most breathtaking, picturesque trout stream in the Keystone State? Those few who fish the stream and even the smaller percentage who fly-fish it would agree unanimously that their selection would be Rock Run at Ralston in Lycoming County. It's less than 10 miles southeast of Roaring Branch (see page 71).

Just ask Andrew Krouse of the Philadelphia area what he thinks of Rock Run. Andy has fished most streams in the state and he lists this one as "the most beautiful trout stream in Pennsylvania." Russell Machmer of nearby Canton would agree. He's seen green drakes and light cahills on the stream and says Rock Run and Roaring Branch are two of the most spectacular streams in the state. Rock Run ranges from 10 to 30 feet wide at most places, with some ledge pools as deep as 20 or 30 feet. In some areas you have to search the substrate long for just one pebble or rock.

I recently had an opportunity to fly-fish this freestone stream in late July. During the summer, public camping is available near the stream, so you'll have to contend with some campers and fishing pressure—even in late summer. I waded along the bank and almost immediately fell off a cliff. I wasn't injured, but watch your step along this stream! I did manage to catch a few planted trout—in 62-degree water. Two weeks later I again fly-fished Rock Run—this time a couple of miles upstream. I recorded a temperature of 59 degrees on that late-July afternoon. I caught one brook trout more than 8 inches long and a 14-inch, hook-jawed brown trout that had escaped anglers' bait for at least a year.

Don't expect to see any spectacular hatches on Rock Run. Because of the character of the stream and substrate, hatches aren't as heavy as you'd expect.

You can reach the stream off PA 14 about 15 miles north of Williamsport. At the town of Ralston, take the dirt road (Rock Run Road) heading east and paralleling the stream. You'll find several pulloff areas along this road. Reach the upper end of Rock Run via SR 1013, just north of Ellenton.

BEST TIMES TO FLY-FISH

April 10–May 10
Quill gordon: afternoon, size 14
Blue quill: afternoon, size 18
Light stonefly: afternoon, size 14

May 11–June 30
Sulphur: evening, size 16 or 18
March brown/gray fox: afternoon, size 12
Light cahill: evening, size 14
Early brown stonefly: afternoon, size 14
Blue quill: morning, size 18
Green drake: evening, size 12 (spotty)
Little yellow stonefly: afternoon and evening, size 16
Little green stonefly: afternoon and evening, size 16

12. PLEASANT STREAM

Rating: 7   DeLorme map: 50

Positives: *Plenty of stream to fly-fish • Good hatches • Native and streambred trout • Easy access*
Negatives: *Poor road on upper end • Stream habitat destroyed in places*

Boy! Does this name fit this trout stream! It's a beautiful freestone stream that, after a 12-mile journey, enters Lycoming Creek at the village of Marsh Hill. But the residents who own homes and cabins along Pleasant Stream might not agree with the name—at least not always. On January 20, 1996, Pleasant Stream poured over its banks and into many of the cabins lining the lower end of the stream. That winter flood ruined much of the road that closely parallels the stream—so much so that the Fish and Boat Commission didn't stock the stream in 1996. The flood also ruined substrate and dislodged many of the aquatic insects.

Despite that tremendous devastation, Pleasant Stream still has a good native population of brook trout and streambred brown trout. In fact, I've caught even small rainbows on the stream that look streambred. Local angler Russell Machmer says he too catches streambred rainbows on some of the area water.

Anglers will find four tributaries to Lycoming Creek along PA 14 that are excellent and productive trout streams. I covered Grays Run, the southernmost, in *Pennsylvania Trout Streams and Their Hatches*. Starting at the northern end, Roaring Branch (see page 71) empties into Lycoming first. It's difficult to access, and once you are on this 15- to 20-foot-wide stream you'll have a problem moving freely up- and downstream because of huge boulders in the flow. Rock Run (see page 73) enters next. This is the most picturesque stream I have ever fly-fished in Pennsylvania. It has huge ledges and deep pools—with few stones and gravel. Pleasant Stream enters about 4 miles downstream from Rock Run. Of the four, Pleasant Stream looks most like the typical freestone mountain trout stream of Pennsylvania. Pleasant Stream and Rock Run enter from the east, Roaring Branch and Grays Run from the west.

Each time I visit this stream I'm amazed at the extremely clear, cool water. It reminds me of the days I fly-fished on New Zealand trout streams. But the stream still suffers from the effects of the flood, and it will for a long time to come. Depending on when you read this, you can travel along the road next to the stream (Pleasant Stream Road) and readily see the effects. In sections bulldozers have scoured the stream and destroyed any livable habitat for trout and aquatic insects alike. Upstream a few miles the dirt road becomes extremely rutted and is in poor condition—in fact, 3 miles upstream from Marsh Hill the township has closed the road.

Pleasant Stream ranges from 15 to 25 feet wide and has some fairly deep pools and productive riffles. You'll find temperatures on the stream

A site on Pleasant Stream has been excavated by the 1996 flood.

in the low 60s even in late summer. I checked the temperature one August morning and got a reading of 61 degrees.

You'll find hatches on Pleasant Stream even into late summer. In July and August you'll find blue quills and blue-winged olive duns on the surface. Earlier, in April, the stream hosts the usual array of mayflies, including the quill gordon, blue quill, and hendrickson.

BEST TIMES TO FLY-FISH

April 10–May 10
Blue quill: afternoon, size 18
Quill gordon: afternoon, size 14
Hendrickson: afternoon, size 14
Grannom: afternoon, size 16

May 11–June 30
Light stonefly: afternoon, size 14
March brown/gray fox: afternoon, size 14
Sulphur: evening, size 16 or 18
Light cahill: evening, size 14
Green drake: evening, size 12 (spotty)
Blue quill: morning, size 18
Blue-winged olive dun: morning, size 14
Little yellow stonefly: evening, size 16
Little green stonefly: evening, size 18
Slate drake: evening, size 14

July 1–August 31
Blue quill: morning, size 18
Blue-winged olive dun: morning, size 16 or 18
Dark gray stonefly: morning, size 18
Slate drake: evening, size 14

September 1–October 31
Slate drake: afternoon, size 14

13. MEDIX RUN

Rating: 5   DeLorme map: 47

Positives: *Native and streambred trout • Stream improvements*
• Easily accessible (also a negative)
Negatives: *Heavily fished at the beginning of the season and on holidays*

Someone should erect a historical sign or marker on Medix Run, which is just about 30 miles northeast of DuBois, Pennsylvania. George Harvey, the dean of American fly-fishers, cut his teeth on this small but productive trout stream. George still has fond memories of this 15- to 25-foot-wide freestone stream. He started fly-fishing on it back in the early 1900s and still vividly recalls those train rides he had to take to reach the stream. Even now in his later years he can remember some of the hatches he fished on this stream, like the green drake and the quill gordon. If you travel the road along the stream, you'll still see the Harvey Camp, where Little Medix joins the main stem. That's where George stayed while fly-fishing here.

Because an improved dirt road runs along Medix Run and its two major tributaries, this stream gets a lot of angling pressure. "I've seen as many as 100 cars parked along the stream on opening day," laments Doug Challingsworth of Weedville. After Memorial Day the crowds thin out and you'll find few fly-fishers on the stream.

Late fall on Medix Run in north-central Pennsylvania

Pennsylvania Wildlife Habitat Unlimited has taken an active role in preserving Medix Run. Annually the group undertakes a project to improve the stream. Projects to date include the construction of jack dams and stream erosion control. If you plan to or if you already do fly-fish this stream, this organization needs your help.

Recently Craig Josephson, Eddie Miloser of Glen Campbell, Pennsylvania, and I spent a half day on Medix Run. We chose the wrong day. It was the Saturday just before Memorial Day. Why was that date so bad? You'll find plenty of hunting and fishing camps within a few miles of Medix Run, and each had a crowd for that long weekend. Dozens of campers filled the stream that afternoon. If you plan to fly-fish Medix Run, avoid it near opening day and on any holiday.

Despite the heavy fishing pressure, Medix Run showed us some of its trout and a few of its mayflies. In about 2 hours of fly-fishing in bright sunlight on a late-May afternoon, the three of us caught a half-dozen trout on size-16 Bead Head Pheasant Tail Nymphs.

John Palumbo of nearby Pennfield is one of those local anglers who fly-fishes Medix Run often. He uses a version of the Slate Drake or Adams he calls the Palumbo Special. He's caught plenty of trout on that gray-bodied pattern on Medix. Gerald Bortz, an expert fly-tier and fly-fisher from nearby DuBois, also fishes on the stream frequently. He's seen some hendricksons on Medix but prefers to use caddis imitations.

Little Medix Run joins the main stem about 5 miles upstream. One afternoon several years ago, Craig Josephson put on a fly-fishing clinic on this small stream. In less than 100 feet of Little Medix, he landed a dozen brook trout.

Medix Run also holds a good population of native brook trout, along with planted brown trout. PA 555 gets you to the lower end of Medix Run. SR 2004 (blacktop) and then Medix Grade Road (dirt) closely parallel much of the stream. Little Medix Road follows one of the two major tributaries. Jack Dent Road (off Medix Grade Road) follows the other branch. There are 10 miles of good fly-fishing on the main stem of this small mountain stream and several miles on each of the two tributaries.

Medix Run holds several refuge areas where there's no fishing allowed before June 15. These serve as safe havens for trout. These sections are well marked and spread throughout much of the stream.

Medix Run eventually flows into the highly polluted Bennett Branch of the Sinnemahoning at the town of Medix Run. Still, if you're a small-stream aficionado, you'll really enjoy fly-fishing this one. Even though it's small, it's not difficult to fly-fish.

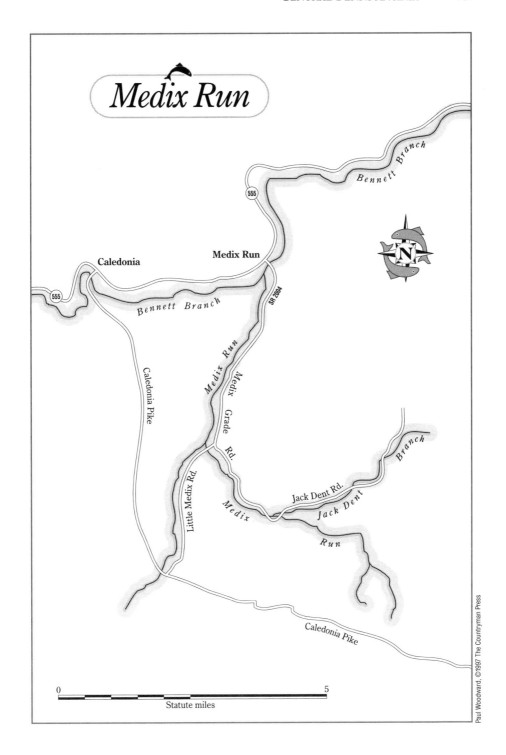

Medix Run

Caledonia

Medix Run

555

555

Bennett Branch

Bennett Branch

SR 2004

N

Caledonia Pike

Medix Run

Medix Grade Rd.

Little Medix Rd.

Jack Dent Rd.

Jack Dent Branch

Medix Run

Caledonia Pike

0   5

Statute miles

And if you do happen to fly-fish on Medix Run, remember the good old days—the days before cars became common and ordinary—the days of the late 1800s and early 1900s when anglers traveled by train to reach some of our better trout streams. Remember also that the master of fly-fishing, George Harvey, may have cast his first dry fly right where you're standing now.

BEST TIMES TO FLY-FISH

April 10–May 10
Blue quill: afternoon, size 18
Quill gordon: afternoon, size 14
Hendrickson: afternoon, size 14 or 16
Early brown stonefly: afternoon, size 14

May 11–June 15
March brown/gray fox: afternoon and evening, size 12
Green drake: afternoon and evening, size 10
Slate drake: evening, size 14
Light cahill: evening, size 14
Little yellow stonefly: afternoon and evening, size 16
Little green stonefly: afternoon and evening, size 16
Tan caddis: evening, size 14 or 16

June 16–August 31
Slate drake: afternoon, size 14

September 1–October 1
Slate drake: afternoon, size 14
Tan caddis: afternoon, size 14

Bruce Matolyak lands a brook trout on Baker Run.

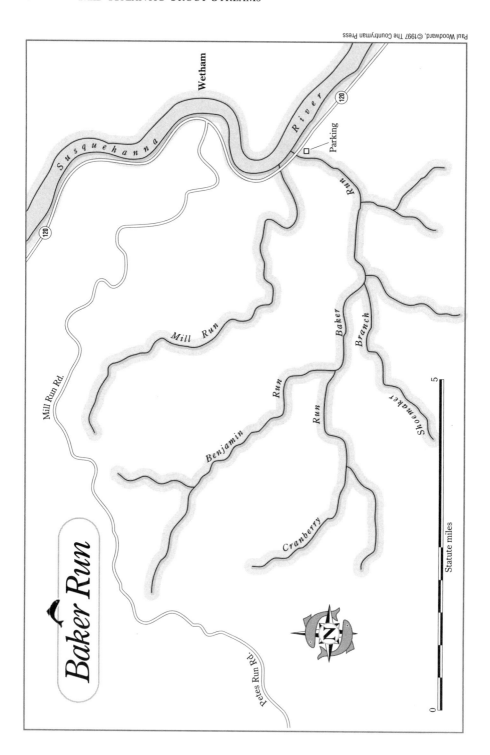

14. BAKER RUN

Rating: 6   DeLorme map: 48

Positives: *Spectacular setting • Some good hatches • Plenty of streambred trout • Isolated stream*

Negatives: *Walk in to reach the upper end • Some pressure on the more accessible lower end early in the season*

At least once a year George Harvey and I crossed Baker Run on our way to Young Womans Creek. Each time we did, one of us would make a comment about fishing the stream some time soon. We never did. Sure, Baker looked productive, but we never really gave it a second thought. We were always in a hurry to reach the more renowned trout stream about 15 miles to the north.

Not until Mark Jackson suggested I try this little gem did I get interested. The first time I fly-fished Baker Run was in mid-April with Bruce Matolyak. Bruce has fly-fished for more than a quarter century. He's taught fly-casting and fly-tying and has worked at Orvis shops in Houston and New Orleans. He's an accomplished fly-fisher, and he enjoys trying new streams. Bruce looked forward to that trip to Baker Run. But on the early-season day we selected to fish it, this small freestone stream was almost overflowing its banks. Bruce and I walked away from the stream after a couple of hours with only a few small native trout to show for our efforts. But the stream and its setting would bring me back several times during the upcoming season.

Baker Run flows through an isolated north-central Pennsylvania valley. It's pristine and it holds several good hatches, plenty of native brookies, and some streambred brown trout. You'll find a parking area just south of the stream on PA 120. Baker flows from west to east and empties into the West Branch of the Susquehanna River about 12 miles northwest of Lock Haven. A jeep trail parallels the stream on the south side, but it's in extremely poor condition—and there are few pulloffs on the dirt road—so the best way to reach the good fishing on this fairly open, small stream is by hiking up the trail. Walk upstream a half mile or more past the cabins located at the lower end. (This lower section does get plenty of fishing pressure; I've seen several bait-fishers there early in the season.) The trail ends about 2 miles upstream, just after crossing Shoemaker Branch.

Early-season hatches abound on Baker Run. I've seen good blue quill and quill gordon hatches appear for a couple of weeks, usually beginning in late April. In late May and early June you'll find some slate drakes, green drakes, March browns, blue quills, and light cahills on the surface.

One early evening in late May I sat at one of the lower pools on Baker and looked for emerging mayflies. In that half hour, from 5 to 5:30 PM, I counted two green drakes, two March browns, and 20 blue quills escaping from the water's surface. Not bad for a small, unknown stream!

BEST TIMES TO FLY-FISH

April 10–May 10
Little blue-winged olive dun: afternoon, size 20
Blue quill: afternoon, size 18
Quill gordon: afternoon, size 14
Early brown stonefly: afternoon, size 14
Hendrickson: afternoon, size 14

May 10–June 15
Green drake: evening, size 10
Blue quill: morning and afternoon, size 18
Yellow sally: afternoon and evening, size 16 or 18
Little green stonefly: afternoon and evening, size 18
March brown/gray fox: afternoon, size 12
Sulphur: evening, size 16 or 18

15. BLACK MOSHANNON CREEK

Delayed Harvest—Artificial Lures Only—begins 0.6 mile below the dam and runs for 1.3 miles

Rating: 4   DeLorme map: 61

Positives: Spectacular scenery • Plenty of open water
Negatives: Tough to fish • Warms in summer • Few good hatches

Look at this small to medium-sized tannin-colored mountain stream, and you would swear that you were fishing trout water in the Pocono Mountains. Not so! Black Moshannon Creek emerges from a lake by the same name in north-central Pennsylvania. It flows through a thick cover of alder and rhododendron—so dense in many areas that it makes casting difficult. You will find plenty of small pools and deep riffles, but there's also much unproductive water.

What about hatches on Black Moshannon? It has a few—especially early in the season. In April you'll often see only midges and orange craneflies on the water and few if any trout rising. By mid-May some mayflies ap-

Black Moshannon Creek in early spring

pear, like the March brown, light cahill, and slate drake. I'm still not certain that the mayfly that appears in mid- to late May on the Black Moshannon is a March brown. The spinner has a yellow body and an orange egg sac. A size-12 March Brown will, however, adequately imitate the natural. Paul Antolosky even reports seeing a few green drakes on the lower end of Black Moshannon in late May and early June. He and his wife, Pat, have actually caught trout on a Green Drake. Still, the main menu item for rising trout is the midge.

You'll find some caddis and stoneflies on the water throughout the season. Caddisflies also make up an important part of the food for trout in Black Moshannon Creek. John Small of nearby Philipsburg especially enjoys fly-fishing on the stream when the tan caddis appear in early June. He's seen trout feeding on these downwings for several weeks.

I fly-fished one early-May afternoon recently and saw nothing on the surface and no trout rising. I recorded a water temperature of 52 degrees and was certain I'd have little success. I switched to a chartreuse Green Weenie because I thought the trout might see this more brightly colored pattern better in the tannin-colored water. It worked—I caught a half-dozen trout on the Weenie in the next hour of fishing!

You'll find 1.3 miles of delayed-harvest/artificial-lure-only water just 0.6 mile below the Kephart Dam. But you'll find much of the better water below the delayed-harvest area. Here the stream widens to 20 to 30 feet and has some sizable pools. I have caught some dark holdover brown trout here. From Huckleberry Road downstream you'll find plenty of sand-

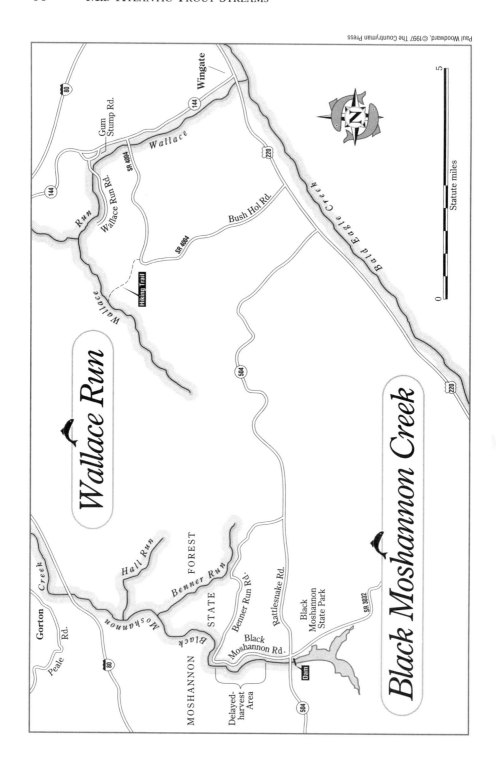

stone springs entering the main stream. These help to cool the water in the summer. Look for trout in late summer just below one of these springs or at the mouth of the Black Moshannon's major tributary, Benner Run. Benner Run itself holds a good population of native brown trout.

You can access the stream at the junction of PA 504 and SR 3032, about 9 miles east of Philipsburg. A fairly good road (Black Moshannon Road) parallels the stream for the next couple of miles. There are parking areas scattered throughout the upper third of Black Moshannon. It's more difficult to reach the lower two-thirds of the stream. A road for four-wheel-drive vehicles does get you close to the stream where Benner Run enters. The lower end of the stream is even more difficult to reach, although you can access it off Peale Road near Gorton.

Best Times to Fly-Fish

April 1–May 1
Early brown stonefly: afternoon, size 14

May 1–June 15
March brown/gray fox: afternoon, size 12
Light cahill: evening, size 14
Slate drake: evening, size 12 or 14
Green drake: evening, size 12 (spotty)
Tan caddis: afternoon and evening, size 16

June 16–July 31
Tan caddis: afternoon and evening, size 16

September 1–October 1
Slate drake: afternoon, size 14
Tan caddis: afternoon, size 14

16. WALLACE RUN

Rating: 5   DeLorme map: 62

Positives: *Some good hatches • Little angling pressure • Lower half easy to reach*
Negatives: *Small • Gets low in midsummer*

For 25 years I traveled along Wallace Run, probably a hundred times—but not once did I stop to fly-fish this small freestone stream. Sure, I had heard good reports about it, but I was always on my way to another stream, and I never seemed to have time to stop.

Andy Leitzinger catches a brown trout on a sulphur hatch on Wallace Run.

Then one day I decided to spend an afternoon on the stream. That first trip occurred in late April. From Wingate and US 220, I drove 3 miles up PA 144. I caught several trout in the first pool I fished. Then I hiked upstream to look for more big pools. On a new stream, I like to explore. I'm always looking for that section that holds a great number of trout. As I headed around a bend in the creek, I came upon a pool probably 4 feet deep and 30 feet long. I saw a half-dozen trout surface-feeding. I scanned the surface; there were equal numbers of blue quills and quill gordons. I tied on a larger Quill Gordon and began casting to a trout rising in the tail of the pool. It took the pattern on the first cast. Then I cast to a second rising trout. It, too, took the imitation on the first cast. I picked up five trout in about 10 casts in that pool.

I hiked upstream for another half mile to the next substantial pool and saw another half-dozen trout working on duns. These trout also eagerly took my imitations. I ended the 2-hour trip catching more than a dozen trout on Wallace Run. Is it worth a trip? You bet it is.

If you fly-fish Wallace Run in April, you'll see not only quill gordons and blue quills but another prolific hatch I call the dark quill gordon. It's an unusual species found on many central Pennsylvania streams; Bald Eagle and Little Bald Eagle Creeks both hold good hatches of this mayfly. I have never seen a male of this species. Greg Hoover and I once examined hundreds of duns on rocks near the water and still never found a male dun. It may be because the species is parthenogenetic—the term entomologists use for species that reproduce without the help of a male. If you look closely in mid-April, you'll often see hundreds of the female duns sitting on rocks along stretches of fast water.

Wallace Run also holds good hatches later in the season. From mid-May into June, this small, fertile stream has a good sulphur hatch, along with some March browns. It also holds some light cahills and slate drakes. Even in late June you'll find good trout fishing over some hatches. Glen Blackwood of Grand Rapids, Michigan, fishes Wallace Run frequently. He originally lived in the nearby town of Julian, and now every time he returns to central Pennsylvania he likes to fly-fish on Wallace Run. He's seen yellow drakes appearing on the surface in late June.

Recently Ken Rictor, Lynn Rotz, and I spent a day fly-fishing central Pennsylvania streams. We first headed to the lower Bald Eagle below Milesburg. Extremely high water levels on this large stream sent us to look for a better spot. We tried Big Fishing Creek near Lock Haven, but found more high water and a water temperature of 48 degrees. So we headed to Wallace Run. Even though Wallace was running high and cold, both Ken and Lynn had action. We saw trout rising to quill gordons for several hours that afternoon—even under those high-water conditions.

You can reach the stream off PA 144 just north of Wingate; it parallels the road for about 4 miles. In the middle and lower parts of the stream, you'll find some streambred brown trout and some native brookies. To reach the middle third of the stream, follow Gum Stump and Wallace Run Roads. The upper third of Wallace Run flows through an isolated part of state game lands. Here, you'll find plenty of native brook trout. You can access this section from SR 4004. It may be difficult to find a parking space near the trail that leads to the upper end of the stream, and once on the trail, you still have to hike in for a mile or more to reach the water. You'll seldom see another angler in this area. In all, there are about 9 miles of water to fish before Wallace Run flows into Bald Eagle Creek at Wingate.

BEST TIMES TO FLY-FISH

April 10–May 10
Blue quill: afternoon, size 18
Quill gordon: afternoon, size 14
Dark quill gordon *(Ameletus ludens)*: afternoon, size 14
Hendrickson: afternoon, size 14

May 10–June 10
Yellow stonefly: all day, size 16
March brown/gray fox: afternoon, size 12

Sulphur: evening, size 16
Blue-winged olive dun: morning, size 14
Slate drake: evening, size 14
Gray drake: evening, size 14
Green stonefly: evening, size 16

June 11–July 31
Yellow drake: evening, size 12

August 1–September 30
Slate drake: evening, size 14

17. MIDDLE CREEK

Rating: 6   DeLorme maps: 63, 64

Positives: *Large water • Good hatches • Holdover trout*
Negatives: *Lower section looks like bass water in summer*

Charlie Wetzel, the great writer, enjoyed fly-fishing it for many years. He saw some great hatches on it. He lived not more than a couple of miles from the stream. What stream? Why, of course it's Middle Creek, tucked away in an isolated valley just south of Penns Creek in central Pennsylvania. Along with one of his closest fishing buddies, Dick Getz, Charlie spent many days fishing the hatches on Middle Creek. His famous book, *Trout Flies,* covers some of the hatches found here. Dick Getz, who illustrated the book, still fly-fishes the stream.

In fact, Dick Getz has a difficult time deciding which hobby comes first—fly-fishing or illustrating. He's highly qualified at both. He has hundreds of superb illustrations of his first love—outdoor adventure. Look at his drawings of trout and turkeys and you too will acclaim his work. But Dick also loves fly-fishing on Middle Creek. He remembers the time he began fishing here one summer. From mid-June through the following year, he caught more than 600 trout on Middle Creek. And hatches—he's seen his share. He's seen trout rising to hendricksons, whiteflies, yellow sallies, and many others. He remembers the time Charlie Wetzel tried to transplant green drakes from Penns Creek to Middle Creek. That experiment didn't work, and the stream still doesn't have a viable green drake population.

Recently I had an opportunity to sit down and chat with Dick and Frank Angelo at Rough and Rustic—an outdoor experience center on the banks of Middle Creek, just outside of McClure in south-central Pennsylvania.

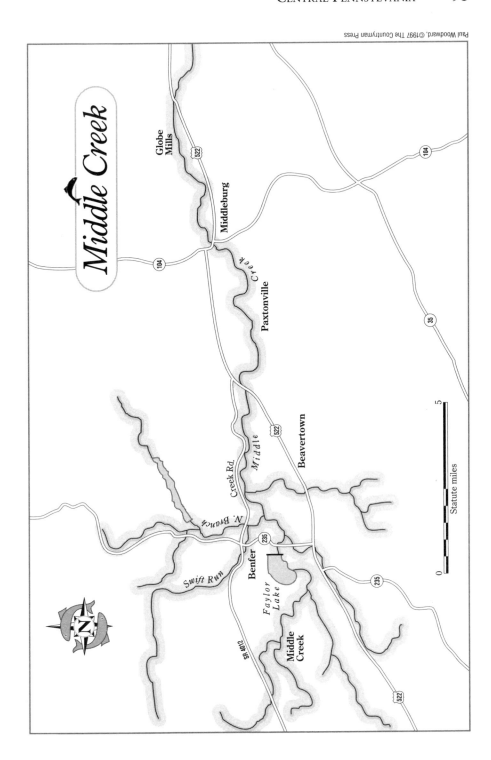

Middle Creek

Frank created this education center for young and old alike to help them experience the outdoors and learn fly-fishing techniques. Both talked about the good hatches and streambred and holdover trout the creek contains. Dick described the time the Fish and Boat Commission electroshocked a section of the stream just below Paxtonville and came up with plenty of big trout. Before then, the commission hadn't stocked that section—but shortly after the survey, it began to stock there. Dick talked, too, about the great fishing in the lower end that he's experienced in September and October—when the second generation of slate drakes appears.

After discussing the stream for the entire morning, Frank finally asked me to fish a couple of sections with him. We first went to the North Branch at Benfer. Swift Run enters the North Branch near here, and Frank and I fished several deep pools on this small but productive stream. We each caught a couple native brookies and a streambred brown trout, and then we headed downstream to the North Branch itself. On the North Branch, even in the middle of the summer, the water runs clear and cool. This branch has a good population of planted trout plus plenty of streambred browns. It boasts a great canopy in much of its flow, so the water remains relatively cool throughout the summer.

At each stop along the way, Frank and I checked the water temperatures. It's interesting to see the variation in these from location to location within 1 hour. Look at the readings we recorded in mid-July along with the location and time:

Middle Creek—100 yards downstream from the Faylor Dam— 1 PM—75 degrees

Swift Run—50 yards upstream from the North Branch— 1:30 PM—67 degrees

North Branch—200 yards downstream from the SR 4012 bridge— 2 PM—68 degrees

Does Middle Creek hold any good hatches? Beginning in April, anglers will find a good hatch of hendricksons. When it rains and Creek Road gets wet, Dick Getz and Frank Angelo have seen thousands of red quill spinners that mistake the road for the stream and hover over the paved highway. But the stream holds much more. Even in late June you'll find some yellow drakes and in July some tricos. But as late as mid-August, anglers can fish over whiteflies on the creek.

What about downwings like stoneflies and caddisflies? Middle Creek has plenty of these hatches. Dick Getz says the yellow sallies emerge in such heavy numbers that they get in your face and annoy you when you're

Frank Angelo fishes the North Branch of Middle Creek.

fishing in June and early July. Even into September and October you'll find caddisflies emerging. This large orange downwing, sometimes called the autumn sedge by anglers, gives trout one last change to gorge on insects before winter arrives.

The Pennsylvania Fish and Boat Commission plants trout in Swift and Kern Runs, both good tributaries; the North Branch; the South Branch; and the main stem downstream to Middleburg. Dick has even heard reports about lunker trout from Middleburg downstream to Globe Mills.

You can reach Middle Creek, its branches, and its tributaries off US 522 between Lewistown and Selinsgrove. Creek Road just north of US 522 parallels much of the stream. The North Branch ranges from 20 to 30 feet wide; the South Branch from 10 to 20 feet wide; and the main stem above and below Middleburg from 40 to 60 feet wide. You'll find some good pools and riffles, with the lower end of the stream (around Middleburg) containing a lot of slow, deep pools. Fish the lower end of the stocked area from Paxtonville to Middleburg in spring and fall. Fish the North Branch during July and August when other parts of the stream get too warm. There are pulloff areas along many sections of the creek.

Where will you spend your fly-fishing time this year? On crowded streams like Big Fishing Creek or Penns Creek? Or will you try a new stream just over the mountain from Penns—one that gets no respect and no attention from fly-fishers—Middle Creek?

BEST TIMES TO FLY-FISH

April 10–May 10
Little blue-winged olive dun: afternoon, size 20
Blue quill: afternoon, size 18
Hendrickson: afternoon, size 14
Grannom: afternoon, size 14 or 16
Black quill: afternoon, size 14

May 11–June 15
Sulphur: evening, size 16
Slate drake: evening, size 12
Light cahill: evening, size 14
March brown/gray fox: afternoon, size 12

June 16–July 31
Slate drake: evening, size 12
Yellow drake: evening, size 12
Trico: morning, size 24
Blue quill: morning, size 18
Little yellow stonefly: evening, size 16
Little green stonefly: evening, size 16 or 18

August 1–October 31
Whitefly: evening, size 14
Trico: morning, size 24
Slate drake: evening, size 14
Little blue-winged olive dun: afternoon, size 24
Autumn sedge: afternoon and evening, size 10

18. MANADA CREEK

*Delayed Harvest—Artificial Lures Only—1.8 miles, from Fogarty Road
downstream to Furnace Road*

Rating: 6   DeLorme maps: 78, 79

Positives: *Streambred and some native trout • Some good hatches*
Negatives: *Some angling pressure • Difficult to fly-fish in upper end*

"Please don't write about the Manada!" That was the sentiment conveyed
to me when I asked several fly-fishermen about this south-central Pennsylvania freestone stream. Does the Manada get too warm in the summer? Is

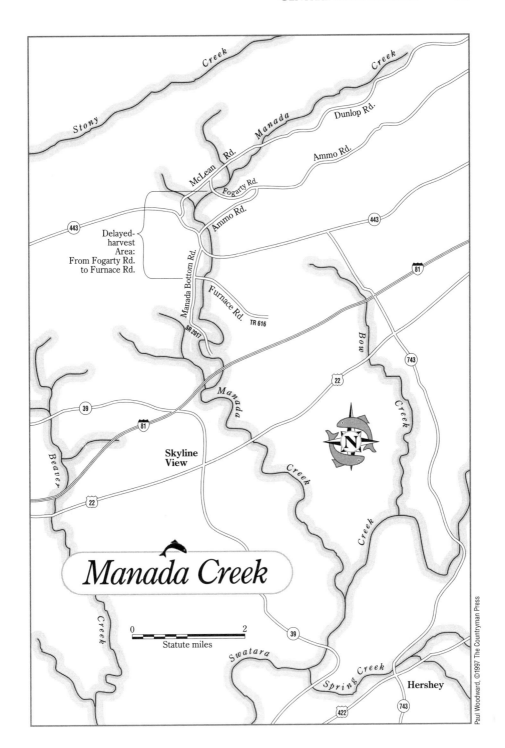

Stony

Creek

Creek

Manada

Dunlop Rd.

McLean Rd.

Ammo Rd.

Fogarty Rd.

443

Delayed-
harvest
Area:
From Fogarty Rd.
to Furnace Rd.

Ammo Rd.

443

81

Manada Bottom Rd.

Furnace Rd.

TR 616

SR 2017

Bow

743

22

39

Manada

81

Creek

Skyline
View

Creek

N

Beaver

Creek

22

Creek

Manada Creek

Creek

0   2

Statute miles

Creek

39

Swatara

Spring Creek

Hershey

743

422

it a put-and-take stream? Does it have limited hatches or siltation problems? The answer to all of these questions is *no!* Local fly-fishers want to keep this highly productive trout stream for themselves. These experts on Manada Creek know how well this jewel of Dauphin County fishes—throughout the entire season.

Dan Schaeffer of Harrisburg is one of the Manada regulars. When Dan isn't winning the Pennsylvania fly-tying championship, he's probably fly-fishing on Manada Creek. He told me once that the Manada has decent brown trout reproduction. At first I didn't believe him, so I decided to fish the Manada several times myself. The bottom of the special-regulations section starts at the Furnace Road (TR 616) Bridge off Manada Bottom Road (SR 2017). This is about 0.8 mile south of the intersection of PA 443 and Manada Bottom Road. This section seems to be one of the most productive stretches of the stream. The delayed-harvest, artificial-lures-only section runs upstream 1 mile above the PA 443 intersection. I fished this section in May and caught several streambred brown trout. These, however, were not the only fish I landed: I hooked and released a mixed bag of larger brown, rainbow, and brook trout. That particular mid-May night the Manada greeted me with a heavy sulphur hatch. Most of the rising trout readily took a size-16 Sulphur Dun.

The Manada does have some problems, however. Most of the upper half of the delayed-harvest section above McLean Road (Fort Indiantown Gap training grounds) is extremely difficult to fly-fish. It will test even the

Manada Creek, near Harrisburg, holds a great sulphur hatch.

most adept angler with its brushy, overgrown areas. The stream narrows from 15 to 25 feet at its lower end to 5 to 10 feet in its upper reaches—you can see why this upper section is difficult to fly-fish. The upper section of the Manada, however, does hold native brook trout. Finally, because of its close proximity to Harrisburg, the Manada does draw a crowd—especially on weekends. This pressure will quickly put down rising trout. If you do fish the Manada over a weekend, arrive early. It's worth the effort. Better yet, fish the stream on a weekday evening. Stop by South Mountain Custom Rod and Tackle in Hershey, south of the creek, and Jim Yurfjefcic will tell you about current hatches and stream conditions. He usually has a good idea of what you'll see on any given day.

The Manada, which is tree lined and well canopied, holds numerous riffles and pools. The Dauphin County Chapter of Trout Unlimited has made several stream improvements. These include stream deflectors that seem to help some of the riffles hold more water. After fishing the Manada, I see why so many wanted to keep this stream to themselves. It's worth a try.

Dunlop Road parallels much of the upper end of the stream and Manada Bottom Road (SR 2017) parallels part of the lower half. PA 443 parallels much of the delayed-harvest section in the Manada Gap area.

—Bryan Meck

BEST TIMES TO FLY-FISH

April 15–May 5
Little blue-winged olive dun: afternoon, size 20 (spotty)
Hendrickson: afternoon, size 14
Blue quill: afternoon, size 18
Little black stonefly: afternoon, size 18

May 6–June 20
Blue-winged olive dun: morning, size 14
Sulphur, dun and spinner: evening, size 16
Tan caddis: afternoon, size 14
Damselfly larva: morning and afternoon, size 10

June 21–September 30
Little blue-winged olive dun: afternoon, size 20 (spotty)

19. CONEWAGO CREEK

Fly-Fishing Only—1.1 miles, from TR 840 to PA 34

Rating: 5   DeLorme map: 91

Positives: *Some good hatches*
Negatives: *Warms in the summer*

I first fly-fished the section of Conewago Creek just above the town of Arendtsville several years ago. The water was well shaded, loaded with stocked trout, relatively cool in the hot summer sun—and private. Few anglers get the opportunity to fly-fish on this exceptional area of the stream. All total, three private clubs own sections of the Conewago Creek above Arendtsville.

There is, however, a delayed-harvest area several miles downstream that is worthwhile. Tom Scow of Harrisburg first told me about this 1 mile of fly-fishing-only water. Tom fishes this section often, and he's impressed with the good number of large trout and the early-season hatches.

The Conewago is about 15 to 25 feet wide in the fly-fishing-only tract and does hold a lot of trout. The Pennsylvania Fish and Boat Commission annually stocks about 800 of them—a mixture of browns and rainbows. Does the project water hold any large trout? Ask Linc Fetters of Arendtsville about the 24-inch brown trout he landed on an Olive Emerger on the Conewago. He'll tell you about some of the stream's lunkers!

Whether I fly-fish the Conewago in April, May, or June, I consistently catch trout. One late-May evening from 6 to 8 PM I caught and released 10 trout. Most of them readily took a size-16 Bead Head Pheasant Tail Nymph that closely copied the emerging sulphur nymphs. I used the Bead Head as a part of a tandem, with a Patriot as my dry fly or strike indicator.

Fly-fishing after June, however, is a different story, especially in the open area of the stream. The Conewago warms considerably in the summer, and without the benefit of many springs or cool mountain tributaries, it becomes a haven for smallmouth bass and sunfish, not for trout.

Where will you find the best fly-fishing on the Conewago? Early in the season, fish the stream between the PA 34 bridge below Biglerville up to about 200 yards below the Russell Tavern Bridge. My favorite section is two-thirds of the way upstream from the PA 34 bridge. You can park along Ziegler Mill Road and walk downstream. (Ziegler Mill Road parallels the entire regulation section.) This section holds many fast pools and riffles, and it seems to be more productive than the water above or below.

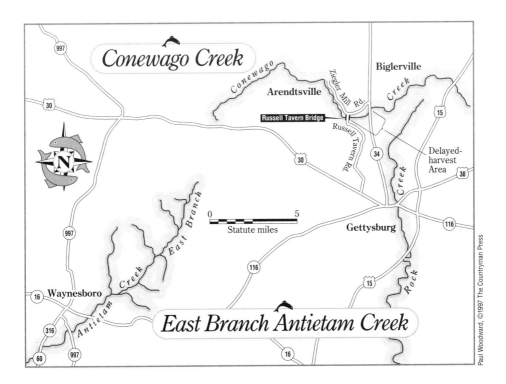

You'll find a good hatch of sulphurs here, and in late May you'll also encounter tan caddis, light cahills, and blue quills. If you don't hit a hatch, try a beetle or ant imitation, or the infamous Green Weenie.

Siltation on the Conewago continues to be a big problem, because there's some intense farming nearby. Many anglers complain that some areas of the stream are not as deep as they once were. Still, you'll see some stream improvement devices. Two Trout Unlimited chapters from Adams County and Virginia undertook the regulated section as a project. It has, however, deteriorated in the past couple of years.

You'll find fly-fishing on the Conewago an enjoyable experience, especially in April and May. You'll catch trout and see some hatches—and few anglers. However, if you travel to this area in June, I suggest you concentrate your angling on the colder streams.

—*Bryan Meck*

BEST TIMES TO FLY-FISH

April 1–May 10
Blue quill: afternoon, size 18
Tan caddis: afternoon and evening, size 14

May 11–June 15
Blue quill: morning, size 18
Sulphur: evening, size 16
Light cahill: evening, size 14
Tan caddis: afternoon and evening, size 14
Slate drake: evening, size 12

20. OTTER CREEK

Rating: 4   *DeLorme map: 93*

Positives: Beautiful stream • Clears up quickly after rain
Negatives: Limited access

"What a beautiful stream." That's what Eric Melby and Jack Ridenour said about Otter Creek, located a few miles southeast of York, the first time they fly-fished it. Set between two mountains, Otter runs from just above the town of New Bridgeville to empty into the Susquehanna River near York Furnace. The character of much of this freestone stream is fast. In fact, you'll find many plunge pools and waterfalls on the lower mile and a half of Otter, especially below Kline Road.

This inaccessibility presents a difficult stocking situation for the Pennsylvania Fish and Boat Commission. In fact, during the 1996 season the commission floated the entire bottom section of Otter (almost 2 miles) with only 200 trout. Once you fish the stream, you'll see why. Many parts are impassable. This is unfortunate, because the lower section is well oxygenated and, with its tree-lined canopy, stays relatively cool. If you fish the lower section of Otter, just before it enters the Susquehanna River, you'll catch mostly smallmouth bass that have come up from the river.

I prefer fly-fishing the middle section. Here, Pickle Road parallels much of the stream. This section is stocked heavily and always seems to have a few brown or rainbow trout holding over. You'll find a 15- to 25-foot-wide stream that contains many pools with large boulders for additional cover. About 0.5 mile below Pickle Road is the Kline Road section with its plunge pools, typical of the lower water.

What about hatches on Otter Creek? Park near the Kline Road Bridge in late April and there's a good chance you'll see good numbers of quill gordons in the faster sections of the stream. The first time I fished Otter I used a Quill Gordon to closely imitate the emerging dun and caught both brown and rainbow trout. That particular evening I even caught two 4-inch brown trout. Along this same area in May, you'll see some sulphurs and caddisflies as well as a few stoneflies.

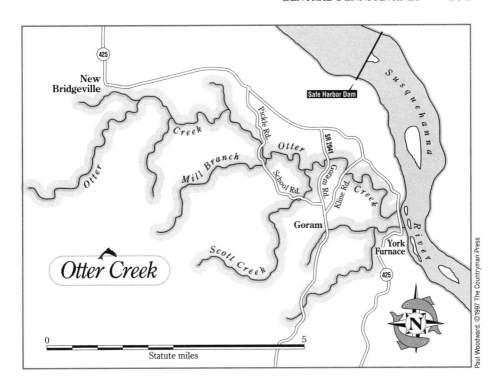

Otter is not without its problems, however. There's no fly-fishing-only section, and the stream gets a lot of pressure early in the season. Certain areas may warm up, and the hatches aren't very heavy. Finally, some sections are posted, and access is limited in upper stretches of Otter. Make sure you thank any landowners whose property you cross, and pick up litter.

Because Otter is relatively close to Muddy Creek and clears up faster after a rainfall, it presents a great opportunity to go to plan B if Muddy (as its name reflects) is high and off color. PA 425 parallels Otter from New Bridgeville down to the Susquehanna River with Pickle, Goram, and Kline Roads all intersecting the creek along the way.

Otter Creek, while not holding over great numbers of trout or having overly productive hatches, is truly a beautiful stream. It shouldn't be overlooked when your travels bring you to southeastern York County.

—*Bryan Meck*

Best Times to Fly-Fish

April 20–May 15
Quill gordon: afternoon, size 14

May 15–June 15
Sulphur: evening, size 16

Eric Melby lands a rainbow trout on the East Branch of Antietam Creek.

Tan caddis: afternoon and evening, size 16
March brown/gray fox: afternoon, size 12
Light cahill: evening, size 14

June 16–August 31
Light cahill: evening, size 14

21. ANTIETAM CREEK (EAST BRANCH)

*Delayed Harvest, Fly-Fishing Only—from Renfrew Museum and Park
downstream 1 mile*

Rating: 6   DeLorme maps: 90, 91

*__Positives:__ Good numbers of trout • Good hatches • Good access
__Negatives:__ Some poaching • Some sections warm in summer
• Many anglers*

Just east of the town of Waynesboro in south-central Pennsylvania on PA 16, you'll cross the East Branch of Antietam Creek. The section located at the Renfrew Museum and Park marks the beginning of the 1-mile delayed-harvest, fly-fishing-only area of this 20- to 30-foot-wide stream.

In the middle of May the stream comes alive with rising trout and good hatches. One evening I saw a large number of cahills, sulphurs, and caddis. That evening I caught eight trout, one of them a 17-inch holdover brown trout that took a Sulphur Emerger.

I bragged about the stream to Eric Melby, Jack Ridenour, and Wendell Blackman, all of the York area, and we all returned to the delayed-harvest area in June. That evening we ran into local stream expert and wildlife conservation officer Jan Caveney. Jan has extensive experience fishing the stream. He favors the middle of the fly-fishing-only section. He especially likes the trico hatch in this area.

But don't worry if you don't see a hatch on the stream. A tandem made up of a Patriot dry fly and a size-16 Bead Head Pheasant Tail Nymph works extremely well on the Antietam. If you don't believe me, try asking Marty Yingling of nearby Waynesboro. He'll tell you about the good number of trout that took one of the two patterns for him in late October. Marty fly-fishes the delayed-harvest area frequently throughout the year.

The delayed-harvest section of Antietam has numerous long, slow, deep pools, along with some deep runs and productive riffles. Above the regulated water, in its upper section, the stream flows much faster and has a rockier bottom. The stream is stocked three times a year (March, April, and the fall) with an average of 400 rainbow and brown trout per stocking. My favorite section is the east side of the upper two-thirds of the special-regulations area. (The lower area, which ends at Welty Bridge Road [PA 997], is slow and is not stocked to the same extent as the upper section.) Two springs join the stream in the fly-fishing section. These coolwater havens save many of the trout during warmer times in the summer. Because of these cool springs, the Antietam holds trout over throughout the year. Unfortunately, according to Jan Caveney, there is little if any wild trout reproduction. Jan says that the tricos on the stream emerge very early in the morning and seldom last for long. However, there are fishable numbers of these mayflies, and the trout do rise to them.

There is easy access on both sides of the stream. Once in Renfrew Park, you'll find many trails that closely parallel the stream. The pavilion area, just below the PA 16 bridge on the east side of the stream, has plenty of parking, and you can work downstream from there.

If you need further information, see George Herold of Herolds Gun Shop on PA 16, about ⅛ mile east of the stream. George has a good selection of fly-fishing equipment and should be able to help you out on current hatches.

—Bryan Meck

BEST TIMES TO FLY-FISH

April 15–April 30
Hendrickson: afternoon, size 14 (spotty)

May 1–June 15
Sulphur: evening, size 16

May 15–June 15
Light cahill: evening, size 14
Gray fox: afternoon, size 14
Tan caddis: evening, size 14
Brown drake: evening, size 10

July 1–September 30
Trico: morning, size 24

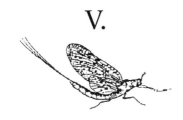

V.

Eastern Pennsylvania

You'll find plenty of overlooked streams in eastern Pennsylvania. Just look at Starrucca Creek, tucked away in the far northeast. Because it flows not far from the Delaware River and New York's Beaverkill, it hardly gets any attention from fly-fishers. And what about Schrader Creek near Towanda? In the past year I've traveled to that stream five times and never seen another fly-fisher. You'll find plenty more quality streams, too, in the northeast.

22. SNAKE CREEK

Rating: 4   *DeLorme maps: Pennsylvania 38, 39;*
New York 48

Positives: *Not heavily fished* • *Some good hatches*
Negatives: *Water warms in summer* • *Few good holding pools*

Walt Carpenter, the world-famous bamboo-rod builder, cut his teeth on this stream. He first fly-fished Snake Creek in 1960. Shortly after that, at age 12, Walt received his first bamboo fly-rod. He broke that prized possession shortly after it was given to him, so he immediately learned how to repair bamboo fly-rods. Walt later made fly-rods for the H.L. Leonard Company. He still makes some of the finest custom bamboo fly-rods available. Recently Walt has returned to his roots in Pennsylvania. Anytime anyone mentions Snake Creek to him, he happily remembers his first few years of trout fishing there.

I wasn't as lucky as Walt Carpenter on my first trip to Snake Creek in northeastern Pennsylvania. I wanted to forget this stream rather than to

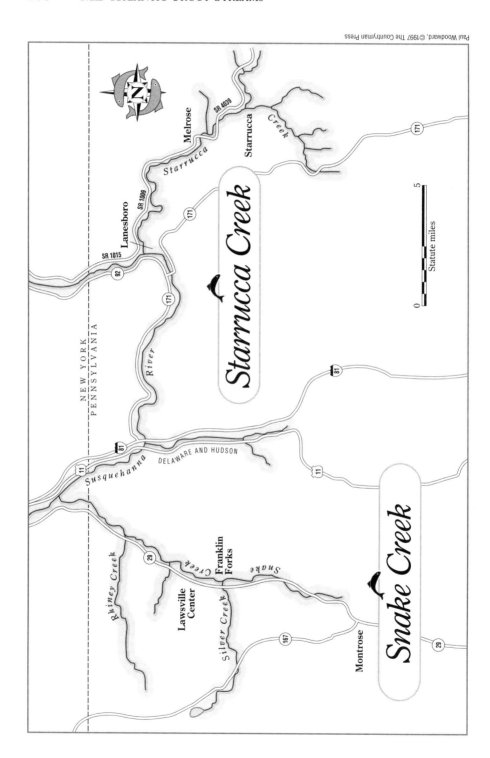

remember it. In fact, I almost quit after a half hour of fishing. Did you ever have a day where everything went wrong? I have had my share of them, but the one I spent on Snake Creek stands out. When I first entered the stream, I waded in over my hipboots. I then began casting to a deep riffle near the far shore—and immediately noticed that my fly-line wasn't casting very easily. Guess what? I'd missed one of the guides. It was the first time that had happened that year. I had to detach the fly and rethread the line. To top it off I did not have a strike on Snake Creek for the first half hour of fishing.

Then I cautiously approached a fairly deep glide partially hidden by overlying bushes and brush. A good place for a trout to hide, I thought. On the first drift through on that productive water, a heavy fish swirled at the dry fly. On the second drift something grabbed my Patriot violently. The fight began—and ended within seconds. The heavy fish broke my 5X leader.

I tied on another tandem made up of a Patriot dry fly and a Bead Head Pheasant Tail Nymph and headed upstream. I fished some deep pools and heavy riffles but didn't have another strike, so I headed back to my car. On the way back downstream I passed the heavy glide where I'd lost that heavy fish just an hour before. I couldn't pass up placing one last cast in that same productive-looking section. The tandem landed almost perfectly under the brush and I watched it float downstream. Within seconds a heavy fish again took the Patriot and headed toward the far shore. After a good fight I landed the 18-inch rainbow. In the right side of the fish's mouth was the tandem that I'd lost just an hour before—in the left side, the one he'd just taken! Talk about a day gone wrong changing around in just a couple of seconds—that one certainly did.

Snake Creek flows through an isolated area just northeast of Montrose. Many sections probably never see a fly the entire year. I fly-fished for a full day in mid-June and never saw another angler—on 10 miles of stream.

Snake Creek holds some good hatches. In April you'll see some blue quills and hendricksons. In mid-June, if the water temperature doesn't get into the 70s, you'll find trout rising to a decent number of slate drakes, blue quills, and light cahills. On just about every exposed rock in the stream, you'll see shucks of the slate drake nymph.

Snake Creek ranges from 30 to 40 feet wide near Franklin Forks to 30 to 50 feet wide downstream 6 miles, near Lawsville Center. If you wade along the stream, you'll find long unproductive stretches with few pools. You'll find some good pools and riffles around Lawsville Center and upstream at Franklin Forks. At the latter village, Silver Creek, a stocked trout stream, enters. From there downstream for a mile or more, you'll find some deep, productive pools. PA 29 parallels Snake Creek for about 10 miles.

As with many of the other streams discussed in this book, you'll find little if any fly-fishing pressure here. If spring and early summer remain cool, fly-fishing on Snake Creek can last well into June and early July.

BEST TIMES TO FLY-FISH

April 10–May 15
Little blue-winged olive dun: afternoon, size 18
Blue quill: afternoon, size 18
Hendrickson: afternoon, size 14
Black quill: afternoon, size 14
Grannom: afternoon, size 14 or 16

May 16–June 30
March brown/gray fox: afternoon, size 12
Slate drake: evening, size 12
Light cahill: evening, size 14
Blue quill: morning, size 18
Sulphur: evening, size 16
Yellow drake: evening, size 12

July 1–September 30
Yellow drake: evening, size 12
Slate drake: evening, size 14
Little blue-winged olive dun: afternoon, size 18

23. STARRUCCA CREEK

Rating: 6   DeLorme map: 39

Positives: Streambred trout • Good holding pools • Little pressure
Good early- and midseason hatches
Negatives: Access on upper end difficult

Talk about overlooked streams—Starrucca Creek has got to be at the top of the list. Like Tunkhannock Creek (see page 114) a few miles to its south, Starrucca Creek loses its identity because of its close proximity to the Delaware River and some of the famous Catskill streams of southern New York. You'll find this quality freestone stream tucked away in the northeast corner of Pennsylvania. Few anglers from the rest of the state experience the great hatches and early- and midseason fly-fishing on this stream.

Ron Payne fly-fishes on Starrucca Creek in August.

Starrucca Creek essentially begins at the town with the same name, where Shadigee Creek enters the main stem. I have, however, heard reports of good fishing above this area. Ron Kozlowski of Nicholson remembers a couple of years ago when he saw a 13-inch native brook trout caught on the stream just above the town of Starrucca. Bob Sentiwany owns the AA Pro Shop in Lehigh Tannery. Bob's an excellent fly-fisher and has fished Starrucca for years. He, too, thinks that there's a good trout population in its upper end.

For the next 5 miles, downstream to Melrose, there's little access to the stream. If you want to reach this productive stretch, you'll have to park your car along SR 1009 and hike a half mile or so into the stream. Because of the lack of access, you'll find few planted trout and very little fishing pressure. You will find some holdover and streambred trout.

Starrucca Creek holds some spectacular deep ledge pools, some heavy riffles, and some good hatches. Any good trout stream has several important features: a good supply of food, some good deep holding water, and cool temperatures during the summer. Starrucca has all three. Add to these little fishing pressure after opening week and a picturesque setting, and you can see why I've rated it highly.

Although the stream holds a great slate drake hatch throughout the summer, Starrucca sees its best hatches in April, May, and early June. During those months you'll find the stream hosting hendrickson, blue quill, light cahill, and March brown hatches. The hendrickson hatch lasts for several days.

SR 1009 follows the stream from Starrucca to Lanesboro, where it enters the Susquehanna River. Below Melrose, access is easier, and you'll find fairly large open water. There are plenty of parking pulloffs along the stream. In all, there are 10 good miles of fly-fishing. Try this one.

BEST TIMES TO FLY-FISH

April 10–May 10
Little blue-winged olive dun: afternoon, size 20
Hendrickson: afternoon, size 14
Quill gordon: afternoon, size 14
Blue quill: afternoon, size 18
Early brown stonefly: afternoon, size 14

May 11–June 15
Tan caddis: evening, size 14
Green caddis: evening, size 14
Blue-winged olive dun: morning, size 14

June 15–August 31
Slate drake: evening, size 12
Blue quill: morning, size 18

September 1–September 30
Slate drake: evening, size 14
Little blue-winged olive dun: afternoon, size 20

24. SCHRADER CREEK

Rating: 5   DeLorme maps: 36, 37

Positives: Spectacular scenery • Fantastic water and deep pools
Isolated and little fishing pressure • Native brook trout
Cool water all summer • More than 10 miles of stream to fish
Negatives: Some acid mine drainage from tributaries on lower end
Ravaged by the January 1996 flood • Few hatches • Recent fish kill

The flood in January 1996 ravaged Schrader Creek in northeastern Pennsylvania. Travel up the dirt road that parallels the stream and—depending on when you read this—you may still see the effects of the high water. Partway up you might see where the high water actually took out part of the road. The flood totally scoured the entire stream. Look in the water and you may

You'll find Schrader Creek in an isolated valley with few other anglers.

see sediment that doesn't belong there. At this writing, you've got to check the stream closely to find any mayfly or stonefly nymphs—many have disappeared. Add to this misfortune the fact that some tributaries contribute acid mine drainage into the main stem, and you can see why it will take Schrader some time to recover from this double-barreled attack.

But Schrader Creek experienced more than just the flood in 1996. I planned to fly-fish a section of the stream just above Carbon Run in mid-July of that year, but as soon as I entered the water I saw dozens of dead fish. Dead trout up to a foot long appeared throughout my half-mile trip upstream. I did not see one live fish in the 2 hours I walked along the creek.

As soon as I arrived home, I contacted the Pennsylvania Fish and Boat Commission about the dead trout. To date I have not found out what caused the fish kill. I hope that Schrader will recover from this latest incident.

I've mentioned throughout this book how difficult it is to locate anglers who fish many of these overlooked trout streams with the fly. Not so with Schrader Creek. George Smith of Wilkes-Barre, for instance, has fished the Schrader for more than 15 years. He has written an outdoors column and a Sunday outdoors page for the Wilkes-Barre *Times Leader* for 9 years and been the northeast editor for *Pennsylvania Afield* since that publication's inception. His work has also appeared in *Pennsylvania Angler* and *Outdoor Life*.

"I used to spend too many weekends on New York's Beaverkill, until I discovered Schrader. For me, Schrader Creek is the kind of water that epitomizes Pennsylvania brook trout fishing. Schrader is what brook trout fishing is all about: pure, cold water; a relatively small stream; lots of rich feeder streams; remoteness; terrific scenery; and the fact that the water isn't usually elbow-to-elbow with anglers after opening day."

Ask George about some of the big trout he's seen on the stream and he'll tell you about the 16-inch brookie he caught with the beginnings of a hook jaw. George says he's spooked trout more than 20 inches long from some of the deeper pools. But most of the fish George catches—and, for that matter, that most fly-fishers catch—run up to 12 inches long. Many of these are native brook trout. George uses terrestrials, especially ant, beetle, and grasshopper patterns, throughout the summer.

What hatches has George seen on the stream? Little blue-winged olives, March browns, and light cahills. He adds that mayfly hatches on Schrader have always been spotty. He thinks, and I agree, that hatches have been reduced because of the water's acidity. The pH (measure of acidity) often runs about 6 on much of the Schrader, and this affects the hatches. (You will see an occasional mayfly, caddisfly, or stonefly, especially in the upper end.) Acid mine drainage enters the main stem from several sources;

two of the main culprits are Falls Creek and Long Valley Run. Authorities plan to install a wetlands on the upper end of Falls Creek by 1998, however. And the Schrader Creek Watershed Association (SCWA) has great plans to restore the stream to its potential. In cooperation with others, it has placed a limestone diversion well on Falls Creek. Jim Walck, a member of this important organization, states that the goal of SCWA is to restore the lower end of the creek to its original state. If you'd like to help, you can contact Schrader Creek Watershed Association, 9 Huston Street, Towanda, PA 18848.

Despite this somber appraisal, Schrader has much to offer the fly-fisher. The farther upstream you travel, the better you'll find the stream. The best section is above Laquin. Just a mile above the town, the Little Schrader, a stocked stream, enters.

Schrader Creek holds a good number of native brook trout. Even in the section below Laquin, I've caught some in the 5- to 8-inch category. If you enjoy a quiet setting with beautiful scenery and few other anglers, you'll appreciate fly-fishing on Schrader Creek. You can access the stream from the lower end by driving up along its banks from Monroeton on Weston Road. You can reach the section near Laquin from Weston Road or from Mountain Road (which soon turns into Foot Plains Road) out of Franklindale. You can reach the headwaters on PA 154. In its upper end, Schrader Creek ranges from 5 to 10 feet wide.

BEST TIMES TO FLY-FISH

April 10–May 10
Little blue-winged olive dun: afternoon, size 20
Blue quill: afternoon, size 18
Hendrickson: afternoon, size 14
Quill gordon: afternoon, size 14

May 11–June 30
March brown/gray fox: afternoon, size 12
Little yellow stonefly: evening, size 16
Little green stonefly: evening, size 18
Slate drake: evening, size 12
Light cahill: evening, size 14
Tan caddis: evening, size 14 or 16

July 1–September 30
Blue quill: morning, size 18
Little blue-winged olive dun: afternoon, size 20
Tan caddis: evening, size 14 or 16

25. TUNKHANNOCK CREEK

Rating: 5   DeLorme maps: 38, 39

Positives: Little fly-fishing pressure • Plenty of water to fly-fish
Negatives: Some stretches get warm

"Few people from Pennsylvania fly-fish Tunkhannock Creek," said Ron Payne, owner of Backmountain Outfitters in Lehman. He's almost dead center with that remark—the only time I used to travel along this northeastern Pennsylvania trout stream was on my way to New York's Beaverkill. Sure, the stream looked inviting to me the more than 20 times I drove along it. Sure, I knew it held some trout. But the Delaware and the Beaverkill were less than 50 miles away, and that's where everybody fly-fishes. Besides, who ever wrote about Tunkhannock Creek?

Tunkhannock reminds me very much of the Genesee River in north-central Pennsylvania (see page 63). Like the Genesee, it has three branches: a main stem, a South Branch, and an East Branch. All three freestone streams range from 20 to 40 feet wide. The state plants trout in all three, but they're not equal in their holding power: The South Branch warms much more quickly than the other two. Look at the water temperatures of all three taken on the same morning in early August:

South Branch—9 AM—Factoryville—67 degrees
East Branch—10 AM—Lenoxville—62 degrees
Tunkhannock (main stem)—11 AM—South Gibson—63 degrees

I've said this before, but it bears repeating: I look for three things when I search for productive trout streams—cover, food, and temperature. The South Branch holds some deep pools and good hatches, but it warms considerably in the summer. The main stem near South Gibson holds cool water during much of the year and some good hatches, but in many areas it lacks the deep pools trout need. The East Branch, however, provides all three ingredients necessary for good fly-fishing. It holds some deep pools, productive riffles, good hatches, and cool water all summer long. As Ron Payne and I fished the East Branch recently, we saw several slate drakes emerge and thousands of blue quill spinners undulating several feet above the stream. Almost every rock along the riffle we fished harbored shucks of slate drakes and Perla stoneflies. You'll also find plenty of caddisflies on Tunkhannock Creek. Examine the substrate and you'll see a lot of the oil-derrick-type cases typical of the grannom, especially in late April and

Isonychia *shucks on the rocks on Tunkhannock Creek*

early May. In September and October you'll find a size-10 brown caddis on the stream.

The main stem of Tunkhannock Creek begins near the town of Jackson in Susquehanna County. PA 92 closely parallels this branch for more than 10 miles. The East Branch joins the main stem near Glenwood. You can access the East Branch off PA 374. You'll find some particularly good fishing areas on this tributary near Lenoxville. The South Branch joins the main stem just below East Lemon. US 6 and PA 438 parallel the South Branch. Tunkhannock Creek flows into the Susquehanna River at Tunkhannock. By the time it enters the river, it's a large, 50- to 80-foot-wide stream. The last 3 miles of this now-combined stream hold a good number of smallmouth bass and an excellent population of hellgrammites.

Remember, you're fishing three separate streams; if you're looking for a specific hatch, you might see it on one of the streams but not another. On all of them, however, you'll find a good supply of blue quills and hendricksons early in the season. If stream conditions are good and you get to the stream in late April around noon, you should see some good hatches on all three branches.

Try this stream—or, rather, streams. You'll find few other fly-fishers. And remember to check with Ron Kozlowski about the hatches on the Tunkhannock. He has a fly shop just 4 miles north of Nicholson on PA 92.

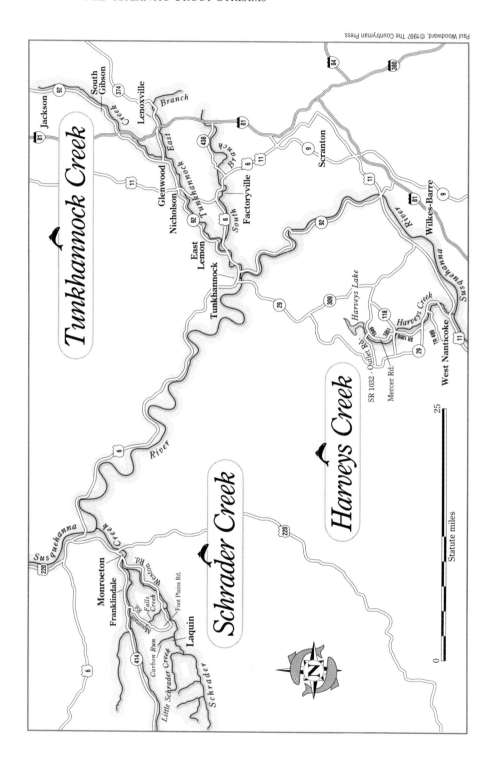

BEST TIMES TO FLY-FISH

April 10–May 10
Little blue-winged olive dun: afternoon, size 20
Blue quill: afternoon, size 18
Quill gordon: afternoon, size 14
Hendrickson: afternoon, size 14
Early brown stonefly: afternoon, size 14

May 11–June 15
Grannom: afternoon, size 14
Sulphur: evening, size 16
March brown/gray fox: afternoon, size 12
Light cahill: evening, size 14
Green drake: evening, size 12 (spotty)
Light stonefly: afternoon, size 14
Slate drake: evening, size 12
Blue-winged olive dun: morning, size 14
Blue quill: morning, size 18
Little yellow stonefly: evening, size 16
Little green stonefly: evening, size 18

June 16–July 31
Tan caddis: evening, size 14
Yellow drake: evening, size 12
Slate drake: evening, size 12
Blue quill: morning, size 18

August 1–September 30
Slate drake: evening, size 14
Blue quill: morning, size 18
Brown caddis: afternoon, size 10

26. HARVEYS CREEK

Rating: 7   *DeLorme map: 52*

Positives: *Some good hatches • Plenty of stream to fish*
Few other fly-fishers • Holdover trout • Plenty of streambred trout
Spectacular pools in middle stretch • Cool water all summer long
Negatives: *Much of the better stretch flows along a busy highway*
Upper end gets warm • Plenty of bathers and parties along the banks

Guess which stream the Pennsylvania Fish and Boat Commission selected for the First of Series "Trout Streams of Pennsylvania" in 1996? It chose Harveys Creek. What? Where in the world is Harveys Creek? It's located just outside Wilkes-Barre in northeastern Pennsylvania.

I had never fished this trout stream until just a short time ago. For more than five years I lived within 10 miles of Harveys Creek. When I fly-fished in the northeast, however, I opted for Bowmans or Fishing Creek. I never heard anything good about Harveys Creek or its hatches. Besides, much of the lower end of Harveys runs next to PA 29, and on any summer day you'll see dozens of people washing their cars and having beer parties along the stream. The atmosphere just didn't seem conducive to a fly-fishing trip.

Harveys Creek empties out of Harveys Lake, the largest natural lake in Pennsylvania. It then flows south for about 8 to 10 miles before it enters the Susquehanna River near Nanticoke. Much of the stream is difficult to access.

It's rare to see a fly-fisher on this stream. Still, two who do fly-fish here are Ron Payne and Don Spencer. Ron owns the Backmountain Outfitters store in Lehman. He's fly-fished for more than half of his 30 years. Recently Ron and I spent an afternoon on Harveys Creek.

We began a mile below the outlet of the lake. Here Harveys takes on the appearance of a hidden mountain stream. It flows through a thick stand of hemlocks and alders, and it's filled with mosquitoes in the summer. On this upper end you'll find few deep pools or pockets. But in much of this area you'll see a relatively slow-meandering, heavily canopied freestone stream. I recorded a water temperature of 69 degrees when we hiked into these upper reaches. After catching only a couple of chubs in this section, we headed downstream to see the rest of this unusual stream.

At a bridge just off PA 118 I recorded the water temperature again and checked the stream for aquatic insects. Contrary to what you'd think, the water temperature got colder the farther downstream we traveled. Just a mile below the dam we recorded 69 degrees; 3 miles downstream we recorded 67; and 6 miles below the dam, 63. Why? Plenty of cool springs enter Harveys on its way to the Susquehanna River. So during the hotter part of the season it might be better to fly-fish this freestone stream's lower reaches rather than its upper end.

As I indicated earlier, that upper end resembles a small, slow-flowing mountain stream. In its lower half, however, Harveys Creek changes character completely. Here it picks up momentum, and here you'll find plenty of riffles, falls, and deep pockets. In this lower half you'll also find some spectacular ledge pools more than 10 feet deep.

The lower end also seems to have more and heavier hatches. Ron Payne says that some green drakes appear around the end of May and the beginning of June. The streams also holds a good sulphur hatch about the same time. Just ask Don Spencer, who fly-fishes Harveys when the sulphurs appear.

Harveys Creek hosts myriad hatches in addition to the green drake and sulphur. Fish the stream in mid-September and you'll see plenty of little blue-wings appearing. Wait until late afternoon and you'll probably witness the rusty spinner, the mating adult of the little blue-winged olive, returning to the water to lay eggs.

What about holdover trout? Harveys has holdovers and there are even plenty of streambred brown trout. One morning in early September, Ron Payne and I caught a half-dozen native brook and streambred brown trout in just a couple of hours. Sometimes in late summer the water temperature can rise into the 70s; but most times, temperatures remain low into July and August.

I've had so much success on my recent trips to Harveys Creek that I've returned again and again. Look at my most recent experience. I fished just below the Plymouth Township Road (TR) 499 bridge one early-August evening. I began by casting a tandem consisting of a Patriot and a size-16 Bead Head Pheasant Tail Nymph. On about my fifth cast into a heavy riffle, a brown trout took the Bead Head and went deep. He broke off almost immediately. I did manage to land a couple of other trout in this section, though, before I headed downstream along PA 29, the busy highway that parallels the stream. In each pool along this active highway, at least one trout came up for my Patriot dry fly. And remember, all of this occurred in August!

Check with Ron Payne at Backmountain Outfitters on the hatches and stream conditions on Harveys Creek. His shop is less than 2 miles from the stream. PA 29 parallels the lower 5 miles of the stream. To reach the upper end, use SR 1059 or SR 1032.

Harveys Creek enters the Susquehanna River at West Nanticoke. Don't overlook the area where the stream enters the river. Ron Payne and I heard an angler talk about seeing hundreds of rainbows rising in this section. In all, there are about 8 miles of good water on Harveys to fly-fish. In its lower end, you'll find many parking pulloffs along PA 29; in its upper reaches, you'll have to park along Mercer Road and walk in.

If parties and people washing their cars don't bother you, then you might be able to understand why the Fish and Boat Commission selected Harveys Creek as the first trout stream of an extended series.

BEST TIMES TO FLY-FISH

April 10–May 15
Little blue-winged olive dun: afternoon, size 20
Blue quill: afternoon, size 18
Hendrickson: afternoon, size 14

May 15–June 30
Sulphur: evening, size 16
Gray fox: afternoon, size 14
Blue quill: morning, size 18
Dark blue quill: evening, size 18
Green drake: evening, size 10
Slate drake: evening, size 12
Little blue-winged olive dun: morning and afternoon, size 20
Light cahill: evening, size 14
Perla stonefly: afternoon and evening, size 12 or 14

July 1–August 31
Green caddis: morning, size 14
Blue quill: morning, size 18
Whitefly: evening, size 14 (at the Susquehanna River)
Light cahill: evening, size 14

September 1–October 31
Slate drake: afternoon, size 14
Little blue-winged olive dun: afternoon, size 20
Cream cahill: afternoon and evening, size 14 or 16

27. POCONO CREEK

Rating: 7   *DeLorme maps: 54, 68*

Positives: *Great hatches • Beautiful stream with plenty of pools and pocket water • Streambred browns and some native brook trout*
Negatives: *Only a few short stretches open • Siltation problem*

In less than 2 hours this summer, Don Baylor caught more than a dozen trout on Pocono Creek during a hatch. Don looks forward each year in late May to the great blue-winged olive hatch this creek harbors. He knows he'll see plenty of insects on the surface and a good number of trout rising to this food supply. He's fished this particular hatch on Pocono Creek for many years.

Don's not your average fly-fisher. He's a skilled entomologist and even runs a consulting firm that works with fishing clubs all over the East. Don and I recently collected several thousand trico nymphs from Penns Creek that he transplanted to club waters near Cleveland, Ohio. Guess what? Several weeks after Don relocated these nymphs, they began emerging in good numbers, creating a decent hatch on their adoptive stream.

Don lives in Stroudsburg, where he teaches English in the local high school. One of his very favorite local streams is Pocono Creek, which flows

Don Baylor shows a streambred brown trout caught on Pocono Creek.

through the center of town. As with nearby McMichael Creek, Pocono has relatively little public fishing water left. But you still can access the stream from Tanite Road and Bridge Street in Stroudsburg and near Bartonsville and Tannersville several miles upstream.

Once on this stream you'll find great hatches and some spectacular stretches of water. Pocono Creek holds moderate early-season hatches, like the blue quill, hendrickson, and quill gordon. Early in the season you'll also see downwings emerging, like the early brown stonefly. But midseason brings on some of the best hatches and the most rising trout. During the morning in late May, you'll find trout feeding on blue-winged olives; in the afternoon, on March browns; and in the evening, on sulphurs. Hatches continue well into the season, and even in late August Pocono Creek displays some slate drakes.

In addition to getting some planted trout, Pocono holds a good number of streambred browns and even some native brook trout. One evening when Don and I spent an hour on the stream, he caught and released a 10-inch native brook trout.

If you like deep riffles, productive pocket water, and fly-fishing in some deep pools, then you'll enjoy fly-fishing on Pocono Creek, which ranks high in my estimation of quality trout streams. It has spectacular water, great hatches, and plenty of streambred trout. What a pity there's not more of this water open to the public. The stream enters McMichael Creek (see below) in the town of Stroudsburg. Even if you have to look for open water or fish in town, this stream is worth a try.

BEST TIMES TO FLY-FISH

April 10–May 10
Little blue-winged olive dun: afternoon, size 20
Blue quill: afternoon, size 18
Quill gordon: afternoon, size 14
Hendrickson: afternoon, size 14
Early brown stonefly: afternoon, size 14

May 11–June 15
Sulphur: evening, size 16
March brown/gray fox: afternoon, size 12
Slate drake: evening, size 12
Blue-winged olive dun: morning, size 14
Light cahill: evening, size 14

June 16–July 31
Slate drake: evening, size 12
Pale evening dun: evening, size 18

August 1–September 30
Slate drake: afternoon and evening, size 14
Blue-winged olive dun: afternoon, size 20

28. MCMICHAEL CREEK

Rating: 5   *DeLorme map: 68*

Positives: *Good hatches • Streambred trout*
Negatives: *Limited fishing • Limited access • Just a small piece of the stream is open to the public*

Here's another example of a trout stream not getting much recognition because it's close to a more famous one. Brodhead Creek flows just a few miles to the north of McMichael Creek and the former, because of all the press, gets all the attention. Still, even though there's only a short stretch of McMichael Creek open to public fishing, it has much to offer.

In fact, some locals swear by McMichael Creek. Don Baylor is one of them. Don should know—he lives just a couple of miles from this great Pocono trout stream. He's fished it for more than 30 years and has enjoyed the great hatches and streambred trout it holds. He bemoans the fact that much of the section still open to trout fishing has been seriously affected by urban development.

Much of what remains public on McMichael Creek flows through the town of Stroudsburg. In town you'll find a 30-foot-wide freestone stream that holds trout all season long. There are about 2 miles of the stream still open. Some of that can be accessed in Stroudsburg off Katz Road and Glenview Avenue. Above town you'll encounter plenty of posted water, but you'll also find some open sections above the Glenbrook Country Club near Beaver Valley Road. The Pohoqualine Club owns 12 miles of the upper end of McMichael. There's little development on this private water, which helps protect the lower end of the stream.

Don and I fly-fished the stream off Creekwood Drive just outside Stroudsburg in mid-September. This section holds one of the heaviest hatches of slate drakes that I've ever seen. Don seined the stream and we saw hundreds of the dark *Isonychia* nymphs that would emerge in the next couple of weeks. Don says this section also holds a great blue-winged olive dun hatch in late May. In late August, a stretch of the lower McMichael has a hatch of the large *Hexagenia* mayflies, unusual for Pocono streams.

McMichael Creek holds plenty of productive riffles and pools and some long, slow stretches of water. Unlike many streams in the area, McMichael doesn't contain the Poconos' typical brownish tannin-colored water. You'll find some stocked trout in town and plenty of streambred brown trout.

This stream is definitely worth a try, especially in late May. It begins west of Stroudsburg near the town of McMichael. In Stroudsburg it picks up Pocono Creek and, finally, flows into the Brodhead. US 209 roughly parallels the lower end of this stream—including the 2-mile public stretch.

BEST TIMES TO FLY-FISH

April 10–May 15
Little blue-winged olive dun: afternoon, size 20
Blue quill: afternoon, size 18
Quill gordon: afternoon, size 14
Hendrickson: afternoon, size 14
Early brown stonefly: afternoon, size 14

May 15–June 15
Sulphur: evening, size 16
March brown/gray fox: afternoon, size 12
Slate drake: evening, size 12
Blue-winged olive dun: morning, size 14
Light cahill: evening, size 14
Tan caddis: evening, size 14
Green caddis: evening, size 14
Pink lady: evening, size 14

June 16–July 31
Slate drake: evening, size 12
Blue-winged olive dun: morning, size 14 or 16
Pale evening dun: evening, size 18

August 1–September 30
Slate drake: evening, size 14
Little blue-winged olive dun: afternoon, size 20
Chalk cahill: evening, size 14
Big slate drake *(Hexagenia)*: evening, size 8

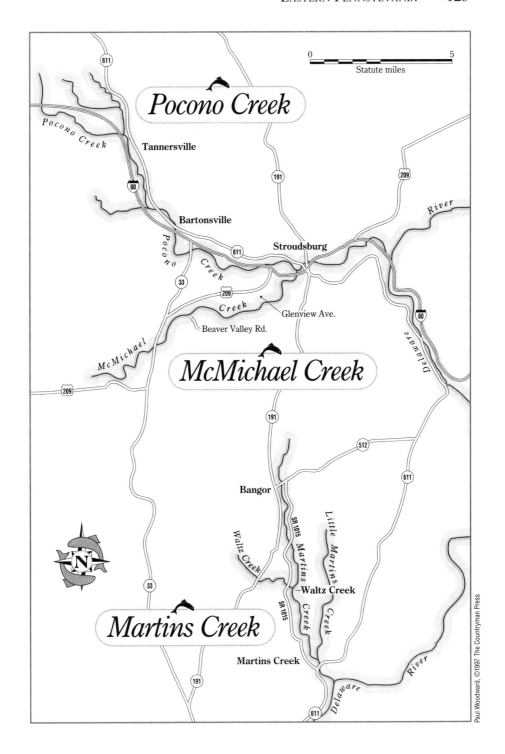

Pocono Creek

Pocono Creek

Tannersville

Bartonsville

Stroudsburg

Glenview Ave.

Beaver Valley Rd.

McMichael

McMichael Creek

Creek

Bangor

Waltz Creek

Little Martins Creek

SR 1015 Martins Creek

Waltz Creek

Martins Creek

Martins Creek

Delaware River

Delaware River

Statute miles

0   5

29. MARTINS CREEK

Rating: 6   DeLorme map: 68

Positives: *Good hatches • Spectacular pools and riffles*
Streambred trout
Negatives: *Difficult access • Some pressure by bait- and spin-fishers all*
summer long

"Thirty years ago you would have seen toilet paper floating past you if you fished this stream," said Al Dally of nearby Pen Argyl. "You would have found trout in this stream at that time, but the aesthetics were something else." Al should know—he's lived and fished in the area all his life. He's fly-fished for more than 30 years.

But times have changed for the better, and Martins Creek has improved tremendously. The upstream town of Bangor installed a sewage plant, and now the stream boasts a great number of respectable hatches; stocked, holdover, and streambred trout; a good cool temperature much of the summer; and plenty of deep holding pools.

This 20- to 40-foot-wide freestone stream, with some limestone at its lower end, begins north of Bangor and flows south into the Delaware River near the town of Martins Creek. There are about 5 miles of good trout fishing. You will, however, find some land posted—although in many cases if you ask permission, landowners allow you to fly-fish.

Martins Creek holds some impressive ledge pools, holes with tangled roots, deep riffles, and productive pocket water. Unlike the case of many Pennsylvania trout streams, you don't have to wade far from one productive pool or riffle to the next. And along the way you're likely to catch some beautifully colored, streambred brown trout. How big do some of these trout get? Ask Rich Keesler, a professional fly-tier, rod maker, and expert fly-fisher of nearby Easton. He'll tell you about the 29-inch brown trout a local caught where Waltz Creek enters the main stem.

Al Dally, Rich Keesler, and I fished a trico hatch on this Northampton County stream recently. Al fishes the stream on a regular basis, and Rich a couple of times a year. When I entered the stream, I recorded a temperature of 60 degrees. Not bad after a week of air temperatures in the high 80s! Rich pointed to a cluster of tricos already in a mating swarm in front of us. As we waded into casting position, we noted a good number of slate drake shucks on nearby rocks, too, and we saw a few light yellow stoneflies emerge from the riffle below us. We saw only a half-dozen trout feeding on trico spinners and only picked up a few streambred trout that morning. But the trout, the hatches, and the stream impressed me.

Al Dally examines some nymphs on Martins Creek.

Several years ago I witnessed an experiment on Martins Creek conducted by the Pennsylvania Fish and Boat Commission and the Brodhead Chapter of Trout Unlimited. On one 100-yard section in the town of Bangor, the group performed no stream modification; on another similar area they constructed log dams and other stream improvement devices. The Fish Commission checked the results two years later and found that the section where modifications were made held more than four times as many trout as the one with no improvements—a great testimonial for stream improvement!

Martins Creek holds some great hatches. Which one do Al and Rich most look forward to? Both suggest you hit the stream near the end of May, when a heavy sulphur dun and spinner fall occurs. But Martins holds many more hatches than just the sulphur and trico. You'll even find the huge *Hexagenia* species and a smaller blue quill on the stream in late August.

There are about 5 miles of good fishing on this stream. Remember, access is difficult and some of the land is posted. If you're uncertain, ask permission before crossing anyone's land. SR 1015 follows the stream from the town of Martins Creek upstream to Bangor. Rich Keesler likes to fly-fish the lower mile of the stream before it enters the Delaware River. Al Dally adds that the section in the town of Bangor get little pressure from anglers. For most of you who live in New Jersey and southeastern Pennsylvania, Martins Creek is less than an hour away—and well worth a trip.

BEST TIMES TO FLY-FISH

April 10–May 11
Little blue-winged olive dun: afternoon, size 20
Blue quill: afternoon, size 18
Hendrickson: afternoon, size 14
Little black stonefly: afternoon, size 16
Early brown stonefly: afternoon, size 14

May 12–June 30
Sulphur: evening, size 16
March brown/gray fox: afternoon, size 12
Blue-winged olive dun: morning, size 14
Slate drake: evening, size 12
Light cahill: evening, size 14
Little yellow stonefly: evening, size 16
Little green stonefly: evening, size 16
Blue quill: morning, size 18

July 1–August 31
Slate drake: evening, size 12
Blue quill: morning, size 18
Trico: morning, size 24
Cream cahill: evening, size 16
Light yellow stonefly: evening, size 14
Big slate drake *(Hexagenia):* evening, size 8
Dark gray stonefly: evening, size 18

September 1–September 30
Little blue-winged olive dun: afternoon, size 20
Trico: morning, size 24
Slate drake: afternoon, size 14
Blue quill: morning, size 18

30. BEAR CREEK

*Delayed Harvest, Artificial Lures Only—1.9 miles, from 800 yards above
TR 662 downstream to the TR 676 bridge*

Rating: 5   DeLorme map: 66

Positives: *A wide diversity of hatches • Some native trout*
Negatives: *Some poaching*

Talk about streams that hold great memories—Bear Creek in Schuylkill
County holds plenty of them for Todd Seigfried and me. I first fly-fished
this southeastern freestone stream more than 50 years ago. I had an entire
section of Bear Creek to myself for several weeks. I caught some of my
first trout on a Yellow Sally there. Yes, I still remember the fly, the trout,
and the place where I caught it. I learned conservation at an early age and
returned that and all my trout to the stream to catch another time.

Later, when I was a high school senior, our local conservation club took
on Bear Creek as a personal project. We stocked fingerling brook trout
and made stream improvements. I still vividly remember those days, too.

Todd Seigfried, fly-tier and guide, has similar recollections about Bear
Creek. Todd's experiences began 31 years ago. He too remembers some of

Todd Seigfried releases a brookie on Bear Creek.

the hatches and successful trips he had on this 20- to 30-foot-wide stream. He has kept a chart of the hatches on Bear Creek for the past decade. Todd has lived within a few miles of the stream for years.

Recently I visited the stream again, with Todd, after a hiatus of 20 years. Joe DeMarkis, owner of the Wilderness Trekker, accompanied us to the delayed-harvest section just a mile upstream from the town of Auburn. Todd and Joe each managed to catch a native brook trout. Each lamented the fact that the stream held few planted trout at the time we fly-fished, in August. Another problem both Joe and Todd mentioned was the poaching that occurs in the delayed-harvest area. And after June 15 it becomes even more difficult to find a legal trout in the stream. Because of a generous amount of precipitation that summer, the stream still boasted some good holding pools and a water temperature of 63 degrees.

Both Joe and Todd recommend that if you plan to fish this stream, you should try it from early April through mid-June. Why hit the stream then? That's when you'll find some of Bear Creek's great hatches. In mid-April you'll witness a respectable hatch of hendricksons on the water, and in mid- to late May you'll find sulphurs on the water every evening. Throughout much of the season, Bear Creek fly-fishers will find slate drakes emerging, and any dark pattern—like an Adams—works well when these appear. Just walk along the delayed-harvest area in June, July, or August and you'll see hundreds of *Isonychia* shucks on the rocks near the stream. But October fly-fishing on the regulated stretch can be productive also. The state usually plants trout in the delayed-harvest section in the fall.

Maybe my most vivid memories of fly-fishing on Bear Creek are of working the section above Summit Station. In its headwaters Bear Creek holds plenty of beautifully colored brook trout. I can remember catching 20 and 30 trout in a morning on this upper stretch. Now much of it is posted against fishing.

PA 895 follows the lower half of the stream from Auburn to Summit Station. You'll find some posted property, but there are also about 4 miles of open water; look for parking in the delayed-harvest area off PA 895. Check with Joe DeMarkis at the Wilderness Trekker in Orwigsburg (717-366-0165) for the latest information on Bear Creek.

BEST TIMES TO FLY-FISH

April 1–May 15
Early black stonefly: afternoon, size 16
Early brown stonefly: afternoon, size 14
Quill gordon: afternoon, size 14
Hendrickson: afternoon, size 14

Spotted sedge: afternoon, size 14
Dark gray caddis: afternoon, size 18

May 16–June 30
Sulphur: evening, size 16
March brown/gray fox: afternoon, size 12
Spotted sedge: afternoon, size 14
Light cahill: evening, size 14
Blue-winged olive dun: morning, size 14
Pink lady: evening, size 14
Gray drake: morning (spinner—evening), size 12
Yellow drake: evening, size 10
Slate drake: evening, size 12
Giant stonefly: size 8 (spotty)
Blue quill: morning, size 18

July 1–August 31
Tan caddis: evening, size 14
Slate drake: evening, size 10

September 1–September 30
Slate drake: afternoon, size 14
Dark gray caddis: evening, size 18

31. MANATAWNY CREEK

Rating: 6   DeLorme map: 81

*Positives: Good access for an urban area • Incredible hatches
Holdover trout and even some streambred ones*
*Negatives: Lots of flat, shallow water • Water warms somewhat in
summer*

Jim Misiura and I selected a stretch of the Manatawny Creek just off
Levengood Road to fly-fish that Saturday morning. Jim had assured me
that this area of the stream contained some holdover trout from early-
season stockings. As both of us began casting to a deep riffle, we heard
music—"Here Comes the Bride"—in the background. We looked toward
the far shore and saw a minister performing a marriage ceremony—right
by the stream! As the two became husband and wife, I hooked a heavy
holdover brown trout. Now the audience attending the ceremony and the

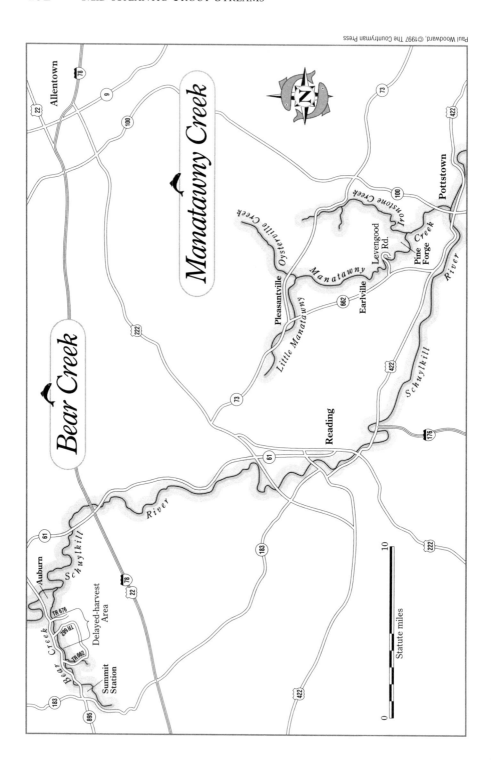

cameraman taping it turned to watch me land the trout. Jim and I quickly made our way upstream and out of sight of the gathering. In my 50 years of trout fishing, catching one amid a wedding ceremony was a first.

Earlier that morning Jim and I met Dick Whitacre and Dave Selby a few miles downstream. Who better to fish Manatawny Creek with than Dick Whitacre of nearby Pottstown? For 60 years Dick has enjoyed fishing on this 50-foot-wide freestone stream just 30 air miles from Philadelphia's Main Line. For years he's looked forward to matching the hendrickson hatch found on the stream. He's caught trout into November on the stream, proving it contains holdovers.

Following the ceremony, the four of us fly-fished for a while just a few miles upstream from Pottstown. It was mid-September—not a particularly good time to fly-fish a stream in southeastern Pennsylvania. Jim Misuira had moved into the area less than a year before and boasted of the great hatches he'd discovered on Manatawny. In fact, just a couple of weeks earlier, in late August, Jim had fly-fished over an incredible hatch of whiteflies. He claimed that hatch was as heavy as or heavier than the one on the Little Juniata River. And just after opening day of the trout season, he had hit a spinner fall of hendricksons. The stream also holds a good number of slate drakes and tricos, and a dozen different caddisflies.

You'll find excellent fly-fishing on Manatawny Creek from Ironstone Creek upstream for nearly 8 miles. And from Earlville upstream you'll find some cooler water and streambred brown trout. Don Baylor has even seen streambred rainbows on one of the tributaries of the Manatawny. Look for some deep riffles, even in midseason, and you'll likely find trout, too.

What a shame this stream doesn't hold a specially regulated area. We caught fish in mid-September, proving that trout *can* hold over during the summer months in this stream. Why not designate an area as delayed harvest, artificial lures only? Fly-fishers could match the stream's great hatches throughout the summer.

And it's too bad as well that some sportsmen in the area don't help float stock the Manatawny. At present, many areas of this heavily bait-fished stream don't get any plantings at all (the state plants trout only from Pleasantville to Pine Forge). Float stocking could help disperse the early-season crowds.

If you're in northern Chester or southeastern Berks County, try this medium-sized freestone stream. You can access much of it off PA 662; Manatawny Creek flows about a mile to the east of that road. Look for pulloff areas next to the stream.

Hit Manatawny Creek when it boasts one of its many hatches. If you do, you too will sing its praises the way Dick Whitacre, Dave Selby, and

Jim Misiura shows off a holdover trout on Manatawny Creek.

Jim Misiura do. And remember, if you hear "Here Comes the Bride," don't be alarmed—you just might land a trout at a wedding ceremony along this popular southeastern Pennsylvania trout stream.

BEST TIMES TO FLY-FISH

April 10–May 15
Little blue-winged olive dun: afternoon, size 20
Hendrickson: afternoon, size 14
Grannom: afternoon, size 14
Blue quill: afternoon, size 18

May 16–June 15
Light cahill: evening, size 14
Slate drake: evening, size 12
Tan caddis: evening, size 14
Little yellow stonefly: evening, size 16
Sulphur: evening, size 16

June 16–July 31
Slate drake: evening, size 12
Trico: morning, size 24
Pale evening dun: evening, size 18

August 1–September 30
Big slate drake *(Hexagenia):* evening, size 8
Slate drake: evening, size 12
Whitefly: evening, size 14
Trico: morning, size 24
Little blue-winged olive dun: afternoon, size 20
Autumn sedge: afternoon, size 10
Green caddis: evening, size 16
Pale evening dun: evening, size 18

VI.

New York Trout Streams

When you think of New York trout streams, what comes to mind? The Beaverkill, Delaware, Willowemoc, Esopus, Ausable, and other Catskill and Adirondack streams have legendary status. Steeped in tradition, these waters lay claim to the birth of fly-fishing in America. They also carry crowds: pilgrimages of anglers who want to fish their legendary hatches or stand in the same water as Theodore Gordon, Art Flick, the Dettes, the Darbees, and others. The renown these waters enjoy came no doubt from their proximity to the major population center of a young nation; their enduring popularity is the result not only of tradition but also of the quality of the experience they provide.

Anglers' libraries are full of books written about these waters. But geographically, their drainages make up less than half of New York State. What about the southern and western parts of the state? Most of the literature in print deals with the Great Lakes fishery. The Salmon River at Pulaski, Oak Orchard Creek, and other well-known tributaries that provide excellent sport for salmon, steelhead, brown trout, and other lake-run strains are well documented.

But southern New York also contains numerous stocked and native trout waters. In this chapter, we have confined our attention to those areas west of I-81 and south of I-90—the New York State Thruway. Characterized by rolling hills, small mountains, and valleys, this area is not unlike many parts of Pennsylvania.

One obstacle to fishing these streams that I have had to become more tolerant of is the posting of private land around many of them. I urge other fishermen to get involved in the situation, as I see it only getting worse over time. One idea that seems to be working in the Syracuse area is a project of the local Trout Unlimited chapter. Many landowners who post land against trespassing do so to keep hunters off their property. When streams pass through this land, anglers must also respect the posting. But many of the landowners don't really object to people fishing these streams; it's just that the generic NO TRESPASSING signs usually include hiking, hunting, fishing, and so on. So what the TU chapter does is approach these landowners and ask for their permission and cooperation in placing FISHING PERMITTED signs, usually right under the NO TRESPASSING signs. This has opened up many areas to anglers that were previously closed. The signs also include admonitions against littering and for the respecting of the landowners' rights. This is a win-win situation!

In the following pages we will cover streams that are predominantly stocked, like the Genesee River, as well as streams that rely on natural reproduction, like the Wiscoy. It may be redundant, but it's still necessary to say: Please practice catch-and-release. It is imperative on native streams, but I feel it is equally important on stocked streams. Freshly stocked trout don't provide the challenge of holdovers or even of fish that have been in the stream a few weeks. And isn't that what it's all about?

Several knowledgeable anglers helped with my research on these streams. Scott Cornett, a region 9 Division of Environmental Conservation (DEC) fisheries technician in Olean, New York, has an intimate knowledge not only of the area's streams, but of their fish and insects as well. Scott was a great help on the Genesee and Ischua. Al Himmel, from the Buffalo area, has been fishing the East Koy and Wiscoy since John F. Kennedy was president. In addition to being a great wit, Al is a devotee of Trout Unlimited and was instrumental in preparing the Western New York Chapter's *Trout and Salmon Guide*. Anyone fishing these waters would benefit greatly by purchasing this book. And a portion of the proceeds go to TU.

Paul Roberts from Ithaca helped with the East and West Branches of the Owego and some other streams I'm not allowed to mention. Paul, in addition to his work at Cornell and his days spent astream, is working with an Ithaca youth organization to open a fly shop in their town. If you are near Ithaca, please look for this shop and support a great cause.

Most important, Charlie Meck helped me, through the use of his knowledge and the value of his friendship.

—*D. Craig Josephson*

32. OATKA CREEK

Special Regulations—Bowerman Road upstream to the twin bridges in
Mumford; open all year, 12-inch minimum, 3 trout per day

Rating: 7   DeLorme maps: 57, 71

Positives: *Cool after Spring Brook enters (never above 72 degrees)*
Good numbers of fish • Good hatches • Oatka Creek Park
Negatives: *Intense year-round pressure • Underwater vegetation, algae*
Posted sections • Clouds up easily

September 9, 1996, started rather badly for Bob Herson of Caledonia, New York. Bob, who is a professional fly-tier and licensed guide, is also a frustrated ice hockey goalie. He left the game that fateful night after giving up an uncharacteristic 11 goals in two periods. Bob, who swears by night fishing, arrived at Oatka Creek Park around 11 PM to take his anger and frustration out on a few trout.

He knew the pool he was fishing in held at least one trophy brown trout—his neighbor told him about it earlier in the season. However, he'd spent the last 15 or 20 nights trying for this lunker, and he was afraid tonight's efforts would be futile, too. Then, using a streamer with brown hackle, Bob hooked what he first thought was a log. Quickly he found out it was his fish. After 15 or 20 minutes, in total darkness, Bob finally coaxed the 29-inch, 12-pound brown to shore. Authorities at the fish hatchery on Spring Brook, a tributary of the Oatka, estimated that the fish was about 20 years old, and streambred! While you won't catch too many 29-inch trout, Bob Herson has caught many in the 25-inch range on the Oatka.

The Oatka basically has three sections. The upper section starts in the town of LeRoy and runs down to the town of Mumford. This area is marginal for fly-fishers—although it does receive a large number of hatchery-raised fish. Spring Brook enters the Oatka at Mumford, widening the stream from 40 feet to 60 to 80 feet. More important, however, Spring Brook carries precious cool water into the Oatka, making it a top-notch trout stream. Spring Brook itself has an excellent population of trout and hatches. Although it's only slightly more than a mile long, about half of it is open to the public.

From the confluence with Spring Brook downstream to the town of Scottsville is the middle—and best—section of the Oatka. The lower section, a 2-mile stretch below Scottsville, does receive quite a few stocked

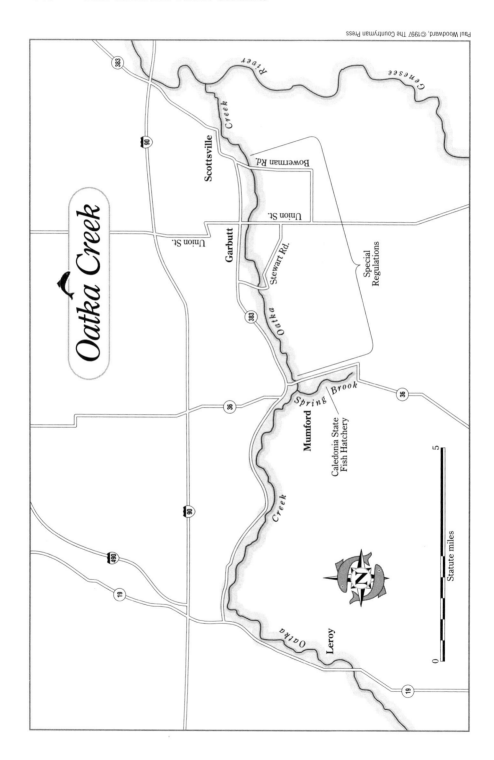

Oatka Creek

trout; unfortunately it warms up considerably in the summer. The Oatka enters the Genesee River just east of Scottsville.

The Oatka does have some private water. The Garbutt Club owns the section between Union Street and Bowerman Road. There are also quite a few smaller posted areas in the middle section of the creek. Luckily for fly-fishermen, the best area on the stream for both hatches and trout is in Oatka Park. There are parking areas along Stewart Road and NY 383, which parallels most of the middle section. Bob Herson and Mike Moeller, a guide at Panorama Trail Outfitters in Rochester, have fished private water on the Oatka. They catch more and larger fish in the park than anywhere on the stream.

The Oatka has great hatches. The hendrickson is one of the best hatches you'll ever fish. Brown and green caddis occur next, usually in early May. Shortly after the two caddis, the stream gets a good sulphur hatch. This pale yellow mayfly is heavy and lasts a long time. March browns, while they seem to have slowed in recent years, can still produce fishable hatches. Tricos and midges finish out the season. You'll see tricos on the water until mid-September.

The Oatka can produce some of the best fly-fishing you'll see in western New York. It can also produce some of the most frustrating. Stay with the park area throughout the year, though, and you should see great hatches and rising trout in the many riffles and deep pools. Call Mike Moeller at Panorama Trail Outfitters in Rochester or Bob Herson in Caledonia if you plan to fish the Oatka. Carl Coleman also fishes and guides on the Oatka; you'll find his shop in Spencerport. All can help you navigate quite a few of the intricacies that the stream and its hatches can present. They can also help you out with stream conditions and what flies to use.

—*Bryan Meck*

BEST TIMES TO FLY-FISH
OATKA CREEK

April 10–May 15
Hendrickson: afternoon, size 14
Brown caddis: afternoon, size 16
Green caddis: afternoon, size 16

May 16–June 30
Sulphur: evening, size 16
March brown: afternoon, size 12

July 1–September 30
Trico: morning, size 24

SPRING BROOK

April 10–May 15
Little blue-winged olive dun: afternoon, size 20

May 16–June 30
Sulphur: evening, size 16

September 1–October 31
Little blue-winged olive dun: afternoon, size 20

33. EAST KOY

Rating: 6   DeLorme map: 56

Positives: *Good access • Cold flow*
Negatives: *Small*

The East Koy—what a fantastic little trout stream! It's a tributary to the Wiscoy (see page 145) and provides some great match-the-hatch opportunities. Brushy willow-lined banks can give the feeling of solitude on this easily accessible stream. Deep pools and riffles provide hiding and feeding places for the planted and streambred trout.

One evening in mid-September, I pulled into the Goldenrod Campground, upstream from the town of Gainesville on Shearing Road. Owned by the Cox family, the campground offers the traveling angler numerous meadow campsites with excellent stream access. After I obtained permission to fish, I assembled my gear and headed down to see if I could find any hatches on this fertile stream. In this section, the East Koy flows 2 to 3 feet deep over a gravel bed. I looked up- and downstream around the brush-lined banks—I was the only person on the stream. As I glanced toward the far shore, I noticed a modest hatch of size-14 caddisflies emerging, and every few minutes a trout came to the surface for one of these downwings. I tied on what I thought was a close imitation and started to fish my way upstream. After about 30 minutes and a couple of brown trout, I noticed a dramatic increase in the intensity of the hatch. When I came to a bend in the stream, the setting sun revealed a blizzardlike swarm of caddis. Fish began to feed on them in sections that I had waded through just minutes before. I covered many of the rises with a Tan Caddis, but few trout struck. Frustrated, I hurriedly captured one of the naturals and turned it over. Underneath the smoky gray wings I saw a dark, dirty tan body—one much darker than the fly at the end of my leader. I quickly hunted through my fly box for a more appropriate pattern. I couldn't find a conventional caddis that matched this color, so I settled for a parachute Adams and hoped for the best.

I quickly cast a couple of feet above the first riser and almost immediately it sucked in my poor excuse for a caddis imitation. I released a beautiful little brown trout, about 9 inches long. Ten more casts and two more fish hit that Adams pattern. The hatch continued with the same intensity, but the setting sun prompted me to consider heading back to the car. With no paths along the brush-lined banks, I decided to fish my way back, throwing slack casts in front of me as I went along. All along the bank I could see fish rising, many of them still anxious to take my Adams. About halfway back to the car, I noticed that its hackle was destroyed, so I pulled it off. For the remainder of the waning evening I continued to fish that fly, now without any hackle—and the trout seemed as cooperative as before. When I reached the campground meadow I looked at my Adams pattern more carefully—I was catching these brown trout on nothing more than gray dubbing on a hook! These fish, I said to myself, are either dumb or awfully hungry.

The East Koy is indeed a productive stream. It has many of the same hatches as the Wiscoy, including the phenomenal caddis hatch I experienced, but unlike the Wiscoy, it's stocked. There is also some stream reproduction.

You can reach the East Koy off NY 39 at Lamont. Take Lamont Road either north or south to access the stream.

—*D. Craig Josephson*

Best Times to Fly-Fish

April 10–May 15
Little blue-winged olive dun: afternoon, size 20
Blue quill: afternoon, size 18
Hendrickson: afternoon, size 14
Grannom: afternoon, size 14

May 16–June 30
Sulphur: evening, size 16
March brown: afternoon, size 12
Green drake: evening, size 8 or 10

The East Koy holds some great caddis hatches.

Slate drake: evening, size 12
Blue-winged olive dun: morning, size 14
Light cahill: evening, size 14
Yellow drake: evening, size 12
Sulphur: evening, size 18

July 1–August 31
Slate drake: evening, size 12
Trico: morning, size 24

September 1–October 15
Trico: morning, size 24
Slate drake: afternoon, size 14
Dark tan caddis: evening, size 14

34. WISCOY CREEK

No Kill—1-mile section near the town of Bliss

Rating: 7   DeLorme maps: 56, 42

Positives: Cold water during summer—upper two-thirds • Abundant streambred trout • Easy access • Good hatches
Negatives: Not many large fish • Some brushy areas

"The flood of January 1996 was hard on the Wiscoy," Al Himmel says. "There aren't the size and numbers of trout that there were before. But they'll be back." Al is a retired schoolteacher and devotes much of his time to Trout Unlimited. He has been referred to as the "Dean of the Wiscoy" and has fished every stretch of it during the last 35 years. Al considers the 1-mile stretch of no-kill water in the town of Bliss one of his favorites. He regularly fishes the morning trico hatch and tries to trick its wary browns with a size-24 imitation.

Al, along with several other devoted anglers and TU members, wrote and published *Trout, Salmon, and Steelhead Fishing in Western New York*. Now in its fourth edition, the booklet gives a section-by-section overview of many of the better trout waters in this region, with detailed maps of each stream showing access points and roads. You'll also find a hatch chart. The proceeds of this booklet go to further stream improvements on many of the waters covered. I highly recommend it for anyone who frequents these

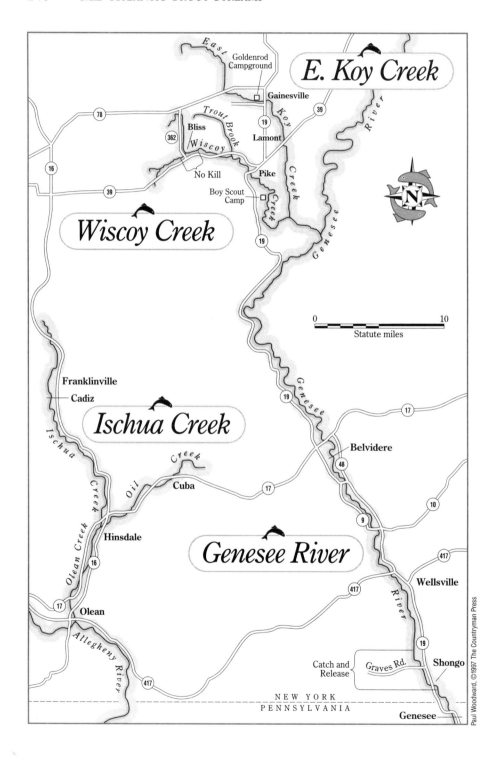

E. Koy Creek

Goldenrod
Campground

Gainesville

Bliss

Trout Brook

Wiscoy

Lamont

No Kill

Pike

Boy Scout
Camp

Wiscoy Creek

Franklinville

Cadiz

Ischua Creek

Cuba

Hinsdale

Belvidere

Genesee River

Olean

Wellsville

Catch and
Release

Graves Rd.

Shongo

NEW YORK
PENNSYLVANIA

Genesee

0   10
Statute miles

Even in fall you can catch trout on Wiscoy Creek.

streams. Most of the western New York fly shops, such as the Oak Orchard Fly Shop in Albion, New York, carry it. It's a must-read book.

The Genesee River System is probably the premier drainage in western New York for the fly-fisher, and Wiscoy Creek enters the Genesee near its midsection. The Wiscoy begins in southern Wyoming County, and the North and West Branches meet at the town of Bliss. It then flows southeasterly, picking up cold-water tributaries like Trout Brook on its way to its junction with the East Koy before emptying into the Genesee River. The Wiscoy is a very clean and productive gravel-bottomed stream and, except for the last mile or so in Allegany County, has not been stocked since the 1970s.

One afternoon in late June, I fished the Boy Scout Camp section east of the town of Pike. This is a particularly attractive stretch for those anglers who prefer solitude; some of the more accessible sections of this stream can get crowded. There are also some nice stream improvements in this area, providing good holding water even for late-season fly-fishing.

As I entered the water at the iron bridge, I glanced up and saw an adult fish fly resting on one of the support beams. This is an easily recognizable "stonefly"-type insect, black wings with white blotches. In their larval form, these large aquatic insects closely resemble a dark gray Woolly Bugger—which should prove an effective pattern on this stream early in the season. There were also numerous slate drake shucks clinging to streamside rocks, with an occasional dun escaping to a nearby tree. I tied on a tandem rig with a Bead Head Hare's Ear Nymph as my point fly, and I cast to some quality runs and likely holding areas. In approximately 2 hours of fishing, I landed more than a dozen browns, three in the 12-inch range.

Upstream 8 or 10 miles, the Wiscoy is very different. In this upper end you'll find a much more open stream flowing through fields. This is prime trico and terrestrial water during the dog days of summer. Although there is posted water, the Wiscoy is easily accessible here off NY 39.

After the January flood of 1996, can the Wiscoy return to its premier status? Al Himmel believes it can, and anyone who has fished it regularly will hope he's right.

—*D. Craig Josephson*

BEST TIMES TO FLY-FISH

April 1–May 15
Blue quill: afternoon, size 18
Little blue-winged olive: afternoon, size 20
Hendrickson: afternoon, size 14
Quill gordon: afternoon, size 12

May 15–June 30
March brown: size 12
Sulphur: size 14
Green drake: size 10
Tan caddis: size 14
Black caddis: size 16
Slate drake: size 12
Light cahill: size 14
Blue-winged olive: size 14 or 16

July 1–July 31
Light cahill: evening, size 14
Slate drake: evening, size 12
Trico: morning, size 22 or 24
Sulphur: evening, size 16 or 18
Blue-winged olive: morning, size 16 or 18

August 1–October 1
Slate drake: evening, size 14
Trico: morning, size 22 or 24
Little blue-winged olive: afternoon, size 20
Tan caddis: evening, size 14
Whitefly: evening, size 12

35. ISCHUA CREEK

Rating: 5   *DeLorme map: 42*

Positives: *Good access • Opportunity for large fish*
Negatives: *Warms in summer • Fishing pressure*

The Ischua begins in a marshy area of Cattaraugus County and flows south, closely paralleling NY 16, through the Ischua Valley. It joins Oil Creek at the town of Hinsdale to form Olean Creek before entering the Allegheny River in Olean, New York. The Ischua averages 20 feet wide and flows through woodlots and open country. The stream bottom is made up of gravel and sand, and it contains a substantial flow, even in summer.

The Ischua contains moderate natural reproduction in the Franklinville area. Scott Cornett of the DEC reports 400 wild brown trout per mile in a section below Franklinville. But the Ischua is primarily a stocked fishery— it receives more than 15,000 fish per season—and is noted for the large fish caught there each year. Scott, who lives near Allegany, fishes it frequently and is successful in tempting the large browns that inhabit its undercut banks. Scott is well aware of the 19- to 22-inch brown trout that his department has recorded in stream studies.

The area above Franklinville is no longer stocked, mostly because of the loss of public access. But anglers who receive permission to cross private lands will be rewarded with holdover and wild trout. The area below Franklinville, down to Cadiz, has good access and stream improvements. I fished this area one afternoon in July; I decided to use a dry-fly attractor in tandem with a weighted nymph because I didn't see any hatch. This section of the Ischua impressed me with its water depth and its pools and bends. In little more than an hour of fishing, I managed to land a beautiful 12-inch holdover brown trout from under a submerged tree root.

Don't overlook the green drake hatch that appears on the stream in late May and early June.

The Ischua is also a good midseason stream. If you hit the stream in the morning, be prepared to match the trico hatch. During the afternoon, try terrestrials.

—D. Craig Josephson

Best Times to Fly-Fish

April 1–May 15
Blue quill: afternoon, size 18
Little blue-winged olive: afternoon, size 20
Hendrickson: afternoon, size 14

May 15–June 30
March brown/gray fox: afternoon, size 12
Grannom: afternoon, size 14
Sulphur: evening, size 16
Green drake: evening, size 10

July 1–August 31
Trico: morning, size 24
Light cahill: evening, size 14
Sulphur: evening, size 18
Blue-winged olive: morning, size 14

September 1–October 15
Brown caddis: evening, size 18 or 20
Little blue-winged olive: afternoon, size 20
Blue quill: morning, size 18

36. GENESEE RIVER

Catch-and-Release—2.5 miles at Shongo

Rating: 6   DeLorme maps: 42, 43, and 57
Positives: Good access • Easy to wade
Negatives: Warms in summer • Little trout reproduction

The Genesee River begins in northern Pennsylvania's Potter County as three inconspicuous 20-foot-wide tributaries—the main stem, Middle Branch, and West Branch. All three branches join near the town of Genesee just south of the New York border. (See page 63 for information on fly-

New York's Genesee River has great hatches.

fishing Pennsylvania's stretches of the river.) The Genesee then flows north and cuts through western New York on its way to Rochester, where it enters Lake Ontario. Although it contains fish through most of its length, trout anglers will do best in the upper reaches—specifically the area upstream of NY 17. The lower section does, however, pick up the flows of several good trout streams such as the Wiscoy, and fly-fishers may do well at these and other junction areas. The Genesee also supports a good population of smallmouth bass between Wellsville and Letchworth State Park.

"The Genesee has a good insect population, but does not seem to benefit from much wild trout reproduction," claims Scott Cornett, fisheries technician for the Department of Environmental Conservation (DEC) region 9 office in Olean. But this shortcoming is offset by a liberal stocking program. Annually the DEC stocks approximately 23,000 brown trout and 6000 rainbows, starting at the Pennsylvania state line and continuing downstream 19 miles to Belmont Dam.

One Saturday afternoon in late July, Scott, Jim Pomeroy, and I met at the DEC parking lot at the Graves Road Bridge. Jim and Scott work together at the DEC office, and both are accomplished fly-fishers. In fact, when Scott's not working he's probably off "playing in the woods," as his answering machine says. Scott averages more than 75 days a year on a stream.

As we assembled our gear, I noticed a swarm of rusty spinners in the air, then a few small trout rising in the pool by the bridge, and my expectations shot up. We proceeded upstream alternating pools, but managed to catch only two or three trout between us on this otherwise perfect summer day. We headed back to the car, dejected.

Then, in the last riffle above the bridge, we saw little blue-winged olives and caddis on the surface. We had to try again—and this time, the section of the river that had given up only one trout 2 hours before seemed to have rising trout everywhere. I watched Scott and Jim catch or hook nearly a dozen fish in the twilight. Our persistence had paid off; it was a memorable evening hatch.

You'll find long, deep, productive runs and some pools that continue for a half mile on this southern New York river. NY 19 parallels much of its cold-water section. Access to the upper Genesee is excellent—above Belvidere, the stream is paralleled by either a paved road or an abandoned railroad bed for most of its length. There are also numerous bridge crossings and parking areas. There is even a 2.5-mile catch-and-release section near Shongo, just a few miles downstream from the Pennsylvania border. Try this one in midsummer for its trico hatch.

—*D. Craig Josephson*

BEST TIMES TO FLY-FISH

April 1–May 15
Little blue-winged olive: afternoon, size 20 or 22
Quill gordon: afternoon, size 12
Hendrickson: afternoon, size 14
Blue quill: afternoon, size 18
Grannom: afternoon, size 14

May 16–July 15
March brown/gray fox: afternoon, size 14
Blue-winged olive dun: morning, size 14 or 16
Sulphur: evening, size 16
Slate drake: evening, size 12
Light cahill: evening, size 14
Golden drake: evening, size 10 or 12
Trico: morning, size 22 or 24

September 1–October 15
Trico: morning, size 22 or 24
Slate drake: size 14
Little blue-winged olive dun: afternoon, size 20 or 22

37. WEST BRANCH OWEGO

Rating: 7   DeLorme map: 47

Positives: *Cold water*
Negatives: *Brushy*

Like an artery flowing through the heart of Tioga County, the West Branch of Owego Creek drains the valley floor and flows southerly before it meets the East Branch. The two continue until emptying into the Susquehanna River at the town of Owego. Access to this stream is almost too good—it's paralleled by a paved road for its entire length. This fertile, 15- to 20-foot-wide gravel stream winds its way through forest and pastureland, bringing cool water to its fish.

Paul Roberts is a research specialist at the Veterinary College of Cornell University in nearby Ithaca, New York, and is an avid fly-fisherman. Paul's education and inquisitive nature have helped him come to know the hatches well. According to Paul, a 23-inch brown trout was observed here during an electroshock survey by the Department of Environmental Conservation (DEC). This would be a fine fish in any stream, but it's an amazing one on the West Branch. Late in the season, few of the pools and runs are

The West Branch of the Owego holds some great brook trout.

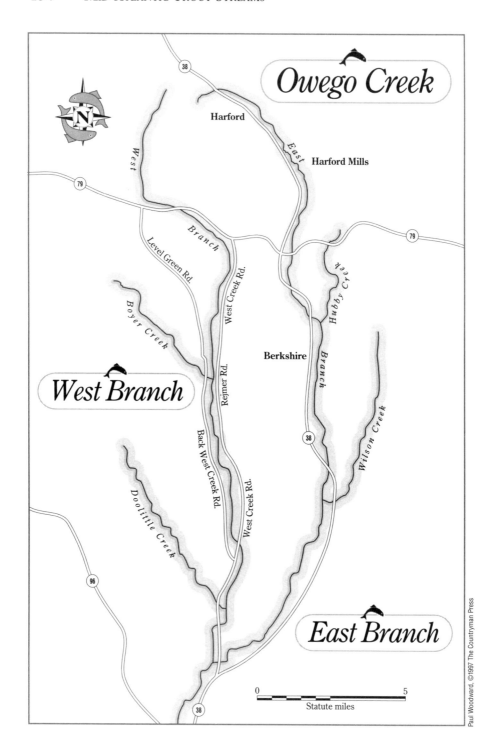

Owego Creek

Harford

Harford Mills

West

East

Branch

West Creek Rd.

Level Green Rd.

Boyer Creek

West Branch

Reimer Rd.

Berkshire

Hubby Creek

Branch

Back West Creek Rd.

Doolittle Creek

West Creek Rd.

Wilson Creek

East Branch

0   5
Statute miles

Paul Woodward, ©1997 The Countryman Press

ever more than knee-deep, but undercut banks and brush tangles provide the holding places necessary for a fish like this.

Charlie Meck and I fished this stream one morning in mid-June. We parked at an access point on West Creek Road just south of NY 79. A check of the water temperature registered 59 degrees. Charlie and I fished our way upstream, alternating pools and runs. Usually one of us fishes until a trout is caught, then turns the stream over to the other. Generally this means that I fish while Charlie takes photographs. Because there are usually few morning hatches this time of year, we fished nymphs and attractor patterns. All of the fish we caught that morning were native brook trout with an occasional brown. In one small run, Charlie caught four brookies in approximately 2 minutes!

When we exited the stream just above this run, we noticed a springhole just a few feet from the bank. The water was in the low 50s. Many similar springs help keep this stream cool all summer long.

—*D. Craig Josephson*

BEST TIMES TO FLY-FISH

April 1–May 15
Blue-winged olive dun: afternoon, size 20
Blue quill: afternoon, size 18
Quill gordon: afternoon, size 14
Hendrickson: afternoon, size 14

May 15–June 30
Green caddis: afternoon, size 14
Sulphur: evening, size 16
March brown: afternoon, size 12
Light cahill: evening, size 12
Slate drake: evening, size 14

July 1–August 31
Slate drake: evening, size 14
Trico: morning, size 24

September 1–September 30
Slate drake: afternoon, size 14
Trico: morning, size 24
Little blue-winged olive dun: afternoon, size 20

38. EAST BRANCH OWEGO

Rating: 6   DeLorme map: 47

Positives: *Good access • Cold water • Large fish*
Negatives: *Heavy pressure*

Diverse is the adjective I use to describe this stream. The East Branch of the Owego begins in southwestern Cortland County, picking up the flows of several small tributaries while continuing south to its junction with the West Branch. Finally the two empty into the Susquehanna at the town of Owego.

While the East Branch contains trout for most of its length, the best fishing is in the upper third of the stream, above Berkshire. Here it runs through an open valley paralleled by NY 38. Averaging 20 to 25 feet wide, this gravel-bottomed stream (with some silt) has several access points and parking areas. There are also some stream improvements in this area, creating a run-and-pool effect.

Farther upstream, above the town of Harford, beaver dams have created an interesting series of ponds, fed by cold springwater and home to an impressive population of native brook trout. Although it's wide open here, the swampy terrain makes for difficult, up-to-your-knees-in-muck wading.

Charlie Meck and I met Paul Roberts of Cornell University at the Richford Access parking area below Harford Mills (just south of Harford) one afternoon in June. Paul likes to fish a small 3-weight outfit on these streams and catches his share of large fish. Paul, in addition to his normal duties at the university, is actively involved in the Fly Fishers Apprentice Program in Ithaca, New York. This worthwhile cause opens the world of fly-fishing to youths in the local community. (For more about this program, see part 9.)

The East Branch receives an abundant supply of stocked fish to augment the native brook and streambred brown trout. The average catch in this section is approximately seven browns for every brookie.

The stream has some impressive hatches, too. On the day that Charlie, Paul, and I fished, we saw spotty emergences of slate drakes, light cahills, sulphurs, and caddis. I hit the same area one morning in mid-August after a major trico hatch and found one streamside cobweb that held six of the small flies in an area the size of my hand! Paul fished a Comparadun and wet-fly dropper and caught and released one brook trout and nine browns, the largest one 16 inches.

—*D. Craig Josephson*

Best Times to Fly-Fish

April 1–May 15
Quill gordon: afternoon, size 14
Little blue-winged olive dun: afternoon, size 20
Hendrickson: afternoon, size 14
Blue quill: afternoon, size 18
Grannom: afternoon, size 16

May 16–June 30
March brown: afternoon, size 12
Sulphur: evening, size 16 or 18
Slate drake: evening, size 12
Blue-winged olive dun: morning, size 14
Little gray caddis: evening, size 16 or 18
Light cahill: evening, size 14

July 1–August 31
Slate drake: evening, size 12
Trico: morning, size 24

September 1–October 15
Slate drake: afternoon, size 14
Little blue-winged olive dun: afternoon, size 20

VII.

New Jersey Rivers

I'll never forget the first time I fly-fished for trout on New Jersey's Pequest River, near Belvidere. Shortly after I parked my car, with its Pennsylvania license plates, an angler came up to me and said: "What are you doing fly-fishing New Jersey waters? You have much better fly-fishing in Pennsylvania—and fewer anglers." Almost the same thing happened a year later, this time on the Big Flat Brook. Another New Jersey angler asked me why I chose to fly-fish in his state.

It's because New Jersey has some good fly-fishing waters—no, some great trout waters—some I consider on a par with many Pennsylvania streams. Consider the Big Flat Brook in northwestern New Jersey or the South Branch of the Raritan River. I believe both of these to be prime examples of top-notch trout streams. Both hold good hatches, streambred and native trout, and plenty of open water. A few Aprils ago I spent more than a week fly-fishing New Jersey rivers. On just about every river I visited, I saw hendricksons appearing. The same can be said for early-fall fly-fishing on the Garden State's trout waters. On every stream I fished in early October, I hit decent hatches of little blue-winged olive duns.

Are the trout streams mentioned above the only viable ones in New Jersey? Not by a long shot. Just ask Russ Kuchner about the Wild Trout Program and the 33 streams and rivers included in it. Wild trout in New Jersey—you've got to be kidding. But fish Van Campen Brook or one of dozens of other good trout streams and you'll no longer laugh at the quality of wild trout fishing in the Garden State.

Ask Russ about the Pequannock River in northern Jersey, too. This tailwater has the potential to become one of the top trout fisheries in the state—no, in the East. All it needs is some cooperation from city officials.

It reminds me a lot of the Gunpowder River in Maryland and the problems experienced where city officials regulated the water flow between two reservoirs. The Pequannock River holds good hatches like the quill gordon, hendrickson, light cahill, little blue-winged olive, and slate drake. It also holds some young wild trout. If authorities were to regulate the water flow and temperature, this river could be a boon to New Jersey freshwater fly-fishing.

We'll examine some of the best trout waters in the Garden State.

39. BIG FLAT BROOK

Fly-Fishing Only—US 206 bridge downriver 4 miles to Roy Bridge on Mountain Road

Rating: 7   DeLorme maps: 54, 55

Positives: *Plenty of open water • Spectacular scenery*
Negatives: *Some posted water • Some pressure shortly after stocking*

Mark Dettmar and Bruce Turner operate the Delaware River Outfitters in Pennington, New Jersey. Much of the time you'll find Mark guiding fly-fishers on one of New Jersey's top trout streams. He's guided on at least a dozen of them. Recently, in mid-October, Mark and I headed an hour and a half north of his shop to fly-fish on one of the Garden State's finest and one of his top choices—the Big Flat Brook. We headed up NJ 31, then took I-80 west to the last exit in New Jersey. There we headed north along River Road. This unbelievably isolated road took us through some of the most spectacular scenery I've even seen—and it happened in New Jersey. Finally, after traveling about 12 miles on this secluded, narrow blacktop, we crossed our final destination, the Big Flat Brook. What a time to fly-fish there! The fall colors added to the beauty of this isolated northwestern New Jersey trout stream.

In the lower area of the Big Flat Brook you'll find a 40- to 60-foot-wide freestone river chock-full of deep pools and runs. You'll see a 2-mile stretch of it posted, but most of the remainder of the lower Big Flat Brook is open to fishing. Sussex County Route (CR) 615 parallels this lower end of the river and CR 640 the middle section.

Upriver, just below US 206, Mark and I stopped for a couple of hours of fishing. From US 206 south you'll find 4 miles of fly-fishing-only water. Here there's plenty of pocket water and the river narrows to 30 or 40 feet. Here and throughout most of the Big Flat Brook, there's a good canopy. This middle section holds plenty of trout and some good hatches. In fact, while Mark and I fly-fished that morning in early October, a decent hatch of little blue-winged olives appeared. And in 2 hours of fishing we caught and released more than a dozen trout.

What about the hatches and fly-fishing earlier in the year? Kevin Wnuck of the Oliver Orvis Shop in Clinton, New Jersey, and I fly-fished the Big Flat Brook one late-April afternoon a couple of years ago, following a morning trip to the Pequest River 50 miles to the south. We headed to the upper end to look for insects and fish the water above a bridge in the state forest. We parked our car, assembled our gear, and headed upstream along this miniature, 20-foot-wide river. We elected to fly-fish the upper section that day, because the stream below flowed with too much velocity.

Would our luck change on the Big Flat Brook? High water on the Pequest that morning had negated any chance for a successful fishing trip. In 2 hours there, neither Kevin nor I had had a strike. Would we be shut out here?

We fished successive pools—I took the first and Kevin fished the next. For the first hundred yards or so above the bridge, we experienced the same kind of luck we'd had for the past couple of days—lousy. Then it happened, at the third pool we fly-fished. In a deep riffle at the head of the pool, a heavy brook trout hit my Patriot dry fly with a vengeance. I landed

Kevin Wnuck fishes the upper end of the Big Flat Brook.

the 12-inch fish and called out to Kevin to show him the first success of the day—no, of the two days. Then I cast the size-12 Patriot into a riffle above the pool—and another heavy brookie took the attractor. For the next hour Kevin and I landed trout in almost every good-looking pool we fished. Finally I entered a 60-foot-long, 3-foot-deep run. I left that same run about a half hour later after landing several trout and missing an equal number. What an afternoon! On that upper end of the river, Kevin and I caught some native brook trout and a few streambred browns. The Big Flat Brook came through for us.

During our time on the upper Flat Brook, we saw hundreds of blue quills emerging, a few black stoneflies, and a couple of quill gordons. But the river also holds hatches throughout the year, like the sulphur in May and June; the slate drake in June and again in September; and the trico from July through September. You'll find the trico hatch on the lower end of the river.

You can reach the river off US 206. North of this road you'll find a small mountain stream. Below, the waters widen to form a classic freestone trout river. Look for parking pulloff areas, especially along the fly-fishing-only section and in the state forest.

How would I compare the Big Flat Brook to New York and Pennsylvania trout waters? It's one of my favorite streams in the East—that should tell you what I think about it.

BEST TIMES TO FLY-FISH

April 1–May 5
Little blue-winged olive dun: afternoon, size 20
Blue quill: afternoon, size 18
Quill gordon: afternoon, size 14
Hendrickson: afternoon, size 14
Little black stonefly: afternoon, size 16

May 6–June 15
Light cahill: evening, size 14
Tan caddis: afternoon, size 14
Gray caddis: afternoon, size 18
March brown/gray fox: afternoon, size 12

June 15–July 31
Trico: morning, size 24
Gray caddis: evening, size 16
Olive caddis: evening, size 16
Tan caddis: evening, size 16

August 1–October 31
Gray caddis: afternoon, size 18
Trico: morning, size 24
Little blue-winged olive dun: afternoon, size 20

40. PAULINSKILL RIVER

*Year-Round Conservation Area—East Branch—from Limecrest railroad
bridge downriver to the confluence with the West Branch*

Rating: 5   DeLorme maps: 55, 68, and 69

Positives: *Some good hatches • Some spectacular stretches*
Negatives: *Posted water • Early-season pressure*

Avoid the Paulinskill River at all costs on the opening day of the New
Jersey trout season. Behind the Blairstown Diner, it's like a zoo. Just ask
John Burke, a local photographer, about the crowds. He takes plenty of
photos of the elbow-to-elbow anglers just behind the diner every opening
day. You'll find these at the Blairstown Diner.

But after opening day, the angling pressure lessens considerably. Kevin
Wnuck of the Oliver Orvis Shop and I stopped behind the diner just a few
days after the season opened and saw only a few anglers. On that late-
April day we also noticed a decent grannom caddisfly hatch appear—but
not one fly-fisher.

In early October I visited the river for a second time with George Slack
of Washington, New Jersey. George has fly-fished the Paulinskill River for
more than 30 years. We headed upriver to Marksboro and traveled down
Paulinskill Road on the north side of the river. This poor excuse for a dirt
road runs for a couple of miles, from Marksboro to Paulina. Near Paulina
you'll find slow water and a dam. In this 2-mile stretch there's some spectacular water, but also plenty of private property. Travel along the river
until you find signs marking the section that's been stocked by the state.
As George and I drove along this section, we stopped a couple of times
and watched several trout feed on the surface.

The Paulinskill River begins north of Newton and flows southwest for
about 30 miles before it enters the Delaware River near Columbia, New
Jersey. The most heavily fished area is from Marksboro downriver. Here
you'll find a 40- to 60-foot-wide river with fast water, slow deep pools,
and many productive riffles and runs. Below Blairstown you'll find access

The Paulinskill River in fall

to the river from Blairstown Airport and Sipley Roads. Look for parking areas along stocked stretches of the river.

Look for hatches on the river early in the season. Hendricksons and quill gordons appear as early as mid-April. Combine these with a heavy hatch of grannoms, and you can easily match the hatch in early season.

NJ 94 parallels much of the river from Newton to Columbia; look for side roads to take you to the water. Will you ever find me fly-fishing on the Paulinskill on opening day? No way! Would I fish the Paulinskill after the crowds have departed? You bet I would!

BEST TIMES TO FLY-FISH

April 1–May 15
Little blue-winged olive dun: afternoon, size 20
Grannom: afternoon, size 14 or 16
Quill gordon: afternoon, size 14
Hendrickson: afternoon, size 14

May 16–June 30
March brown/gray fox: afternoon, size 12
Light cahill: evening, size 14
Sulphur: evening, size 16
Slate drake: evening, size 12

July 1–August 31
Slate drake: evening, size 12
Sulphur: evening, size 18
Big slate drake *(Hexagenia)*: evening, size 6

September 1–October 15
Little blue-winged olive dun: afternoon, size 20
Slate drake: afternoon and evening, size 14

41. PEQUEST RIVER

*Seasonal Trout Conservation Area—from the Conrail bridge
downriver to CR 625*

Rating: 6   DeLorme maps: 55, 69

Positives: *Good fly-fishing down to the Delaware River • Plenty of trout
Plenty of open water • Holdover trout*
Negatives: *Heavy pressure much of the season*

The Bambino—the Sultan of Swat—fly-fished this famous New Jersey river in 1927 and 1928. You don't believe that? Just ask Mario Pasquini, the owner of the Island Park Family Restaurant near Buttzville, to prove it. He'll point to some pictures on his wall of Babe Ruth angling near his eatery. Rumor has it that Herbert Hoover also fly-fished the Pequest frequently. The locals can tell you exactly where the president fished.

Talk about underrated streams and rivers—the Pequest ranks near the top. I talked to longtime fly-fishers Bill Krogh of Kendall Park and George Slack of Washington about it. Bill has fished the river for more than 50 years and has caught many trout in the 5- to 6-pound category.

George has fly-fished the Pequest 30 to 40 times a year since the 1950s. He's seen many hatches and has caught trout rising to slate drakes and light cahills. George's two favorite patterns during the summer are the Adams and the Light Cahill. He's seen as many as 50 trout rising in one evening on the lower stretch, near Belvidere. In late summer, George said, terrestrial patterns also work well.

Recently, George and I fly-fished on the lower end of this 30- to 40-foot-wide river in mid-October. We used tandems made up of size-12 Patriot dry flies and size-12 Bead Head Pheasant Tail Nymphs. In a couple of hours' fishing near Belvidere, George and I caught a half-dozen trout. One of these was a holdover brown trout. Throughout our time there, a heavy little blue-winged olive dun hatch was coming off. Few trout rose to it—one of the last hatches of the season—because the water ran a little off-color and higher than normal.

You'll find a recently built fish hatchery on the Pequest. Take the time to visit this state-of-the-art facility and see what forward-minded New Jersey is doing—and to congratulate the New Jersey Fish and Wildlife Department for a job well done.

As I said before, much of the Pequest is open to fishing. I prefer the section from the hatchery downriver to the Delaware. There's plenty of angling pressure immediately around the hatchery in the area designated

Ann McIntosh fishes the Pequest in April.

as a Seasonal Trout Conservation Area. After late May, anglers can keep only one trout more than 15 inches long in this regulated area. You'll find plenty of good pocket water, riffles, and pools throughout the entire river. US 46 parallels much of its lower reaches. Try this one, and you'll probably like it as much as Babe Ruth did.

Best Times to Fly-Fish

April 1–May 1
Hendrickson: afternoon, size 14
Blue quill: afternoon, size 18

May 2–June 15
March brown/gray fox: afternoon, size 12
Light cahill: evening, size 14
Sulphur: evening, size 16
Slate drake: evening, size 12

June 16–July 31
Sulphur: evening, size 18
Slate drake: evening, size 12
Trico: morning, size 24

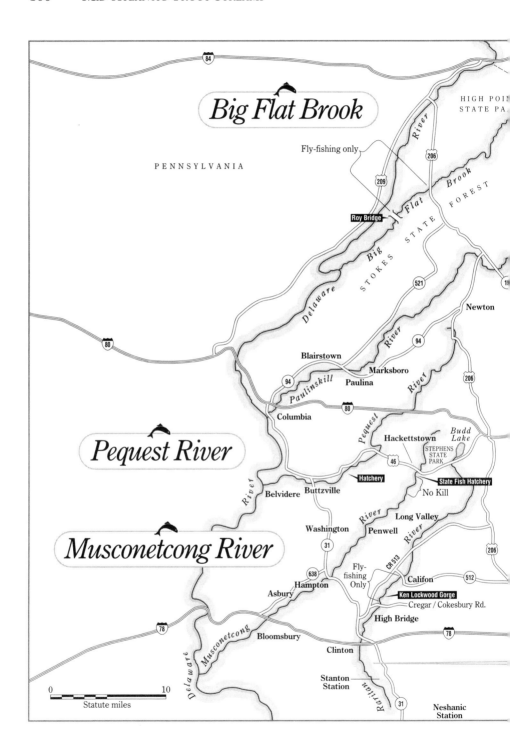

84

HIGH POIN
STATE PA

Big Flat Brook

River

PENNSYLVANIA

206

Fly-fishing only

209

Flat

Brook

FOREST

Roy Bridge

STATE

Big

521

STOKES

1

Newton

80

Delaware

Blairstown

Marksboro

River

94

206

94

Paulina

Paulinskill

River

80

Columbia

Pequest

Budd
Lake

Hackettstown

Pequest River

STEPHENS
STATE
PARK

46

Hatchery

State Fish Hatchery

River

Belvidere   Buttzville

No Kill

River

Long Valley

Musconetcong River

Washington   Penwell

River

31

206

638

Fly-
fishing
Only

CR 513

Califon

512

78

Hampton

Asbury

Ken Lockwood Gorge

Cregar / Cokesbury Rd.

High Bridge

Musconetcong

Bloomsbury

78

Delaware

Clinton

0   10

Statute miles

Stanton
Station

Raritan

31

Neshanic
Station

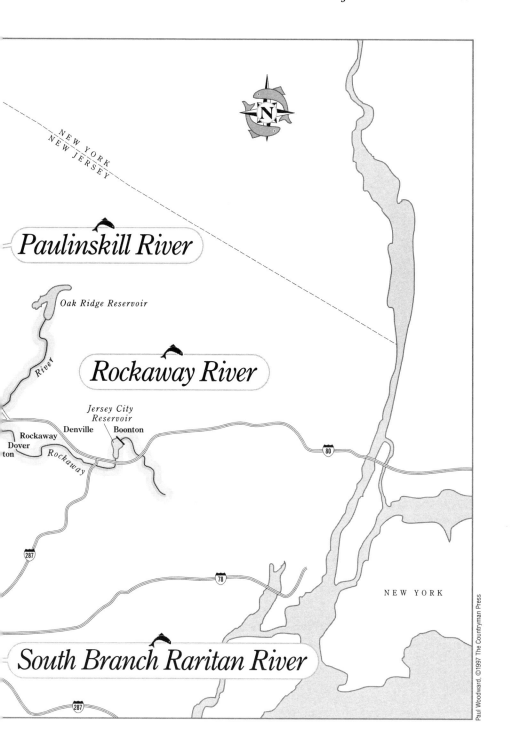

NEW YORK
NEW JERSEY

Paulinskill River

Oak Ridge Reservoir

River

Rockaway River

Jersey City
Reservoir

Denville   Boonton

Rockaway

Dover

ton

Rockaway

80

287

78

NEW YORK

South Branch Raritan River

287

Paul Woodward. ©1997 The Countryman Press

August 1–September 30
Little blue-winged olive dun: afternoon, size 20
Big slate drake *(Hexagenia):* evening, size 8
Slate drake: afternoon and evening, size 14

42. ROCKAWAY RIVER

Rating: 5   DeLorme map: 69

Positives: *Dedicated groups working to preserve river • Some spectacular stretches • Some good hatches • Some holdover trout*
Negatives: *Flows through 15 towns and cities • A "keep-and-kill" attitude on the part of most anglers • Warms in summer*

You'll find good trout fishing in northern New Jersey—and it flows within 20 air miles of New York City. Yes, you read correctly—this river flows just a short distance west of the Big Apple. It's scenic, it has some respectable hatches, and it's got plenty of trout.

"This river's in much better shape now than when I was a kid," boasts Chris Testa of the Morris County Soil Conservation District. Believe it or not, you'll find good trout fishing on the Rockaway River—much of it due to the tireless efforts of some local conservation-minded residents. Chris, along with Randy Brockway of the Natural Resources Conservation Service, exemplifies the transformation that has taken place on this river in the past decade. Randy's and Chris's organizations have worked in a unique way with dozens of local groups to revitalize the Rockaway. Other groups essential in the river's rebirth are the New Jersey chapters of Trout Unlimited (TU), American Rivers, Upper Rockaway River Watershed Association, Morris County Municipal Utilities Authority, US Fish and Wildlife Service, and several other groups.

What happened to the area to create such good fishing in the Rockaway River? Part of the improvement can be accredited to another group called the Friends of the Rockaway River (FoRR). Aaron Sandus is the current president. A few years back, some farsighted anglers became concerned for the future of this northern New Jersey river. Aaron and Sam Sandus of the Hacklebarney Chapter of TU, along with Randy Brockway and others, started meeting and discussing the river's problems and what they could do to alleviate some of them. The group grew shortly into an active corps of 25 to 30 people. What has it done for the river and what does it hope to do? Annually it conducts cleanups of the river. Recently 175 people showed up for one of those planned events. In five years the group has taken 110 tons of garbage out of the river. Additionally, FoRR has planted and reshaped the area of the river around McCarter Park. And it plans to acquire more access sites, create partnerships with industries, and develop planning studies of the watershed. If you ever fish this river—or if you plan to fish it in the future and want to help a worthwhile cause—then you've got to become an active participant in this valuable organization. You can volunteer by calling 973-586-8691.

The Rockaway River flows through 15 communities and more than 12 dams on its way into the Jersey City Reservoir. Add to this dozens of manufacturing plants along the way and you can see why fly-fishing in this metropolitan river will amaze you. Sam Sandus breaks the river into three sections—upper, middle, and lower. In the upper section he includes Jefferson, the Berkshire Valley area, Wharton, and Dover. Here the Rockaway ranges from 20 to 40 feet wide. The middle section embraces that section of the river flowing through Rockaway, Denville, and Boonton, where it widens to 30 to 50 feet. Just below Boonton you'll see the Boonton Falls and Gorge. Here there are 2 miles of spectacular water with huge boulders, some falls, and pools more than 10 feet deep. This section is treacherous to fly-fish at the least, and you should proceed with extreme caution. Sam refers to the lower river as that part below the reservoir. In this lower third you'll find mostly trash fish. In all, there are about 40 miles of river, with about 30 miles holding trout.

Because the Rockaway flows through so many towns and cities, access can be difficult. You'll find parks in Wharton and Denville, though.

Where will you find the best fishing? Aaron Sandus feels the section from Wharton downriver to Dover holds the most trout. Recently the New Jersey Division of Fish, Game, and Wildlife classified 1.8 miles of that section as Trout Maintenance Waters. That means you'll find hold-over trout in this area. This middle section can boast the largest brook trout ever caught in New Jersey. Part of the Morris Canal towpath provides access to some of this good water. In this section the fish and game division would do well to provide an artificial-lures-only section to enhance urban trout fishing.

What about hatches on the river? As we walked along the Rockaway in mid-October, I saw several little blue-winged olives emerge. One, in fact, landed on my notebook! Aaron Sandus said that light cahills emerge in good numbers in late May and early June. Even before that, in April, the river hosts some hendricksons. But, as with many New Jersey rivers, downwings like the tan and green caddis make up the most important source of food for trout in the Rockaway. Aaron Sandus said there are also a lot of scuds in the Rockaway and even some early black stoneflies.

This section of the Rockaway River has a good population of holdover trout.

Remember, even if you don't plan to fly-fish this river, the Friends of the Rockaway River needs your help. With your help and encouragement, this river can continue to improve and become one of New Jersey's better trout streams.

BEST TIMES TO FLY-FISH

February 1–March 31
Early black stonefly: afternoon, sizes 12–16

April 1–May 10
Little blue-winged olive dun: afternoon, size 20
Hendrickson: afternoon, size 14
Blue quill: afternoon, size 18

May 11–June 15
March brown/gray fox: afternoon, size 12
Light cahill: evening, size 14
Sulphur: evening, size 16
Dark green drake: afternoon and evening, size 8
Green caddis: afternoon and evening, size 14
Tan caddis: afternoon and evening, size 14 or 16
Brown caddis: afternoon and evening, size 14 or 16
Slate drake: evening, size 12

June 16–July 31
Slate drake: evening, size 12
Light cahill: evening, size 14

August 1–October 31
Slate drake: evening, size 14
Little blue-winged olive dun: afternoon, size 20

43. MUSCONETCONG RIVER

No Kill—NJ 24 bridge downriver 1 mile

Rating: 6   DeLorme maps: 68, 69

Positives: *Some streambred trout • Good hatches*
Negatives: *Lots of posted land on the lower end*

Did the Musconetcong River harbor any streambred trout? Kevin Wnuck, owner of the Oliver Orvis Shop in Clinton, New Jersey, seemed to think so. Why should he know? Kevin's shop is less than 15 miles from the stream, and he fishes it frequently. He believes that the lower end, near Asbury, has plenty of cool water and streambred trout because of the many springs entering the main river in that area.

I wanted to test Kevin's premise, so the two of us recently fished the lower end of the river. We drove north along the river just 2 miles above I-78 on Warren County Route 638 until we hit an access area. New Jersey Fish and Wildlife is doing an excellent job acquiring access rights to some of its better rivers. The site Kevin and I chose is just one example of its active stance. Kevin and I had only an hour to fly-fish before darkness set in, so we felt a sense of urgency, assembling our gear as we traveled down the well-worn path to the river. Above and below this 300-yard public section was private club water. Kevin says there are five or six private clubs on the Musconetcong, most of them on the lower end.

In this open area Kevin and I fished some of the deeper riffles. After about 20 casts I complained that we only had a few more minutes to fish and we still hadn't caught anything. Then a trout struck my Bead Head Pheasant Tail Nymph. I brought the fish in and showed it to Kevin. There in my hand that evening, I held a 5-inch streambred brown trout. Several casts later we caught another trout in the same area, which also appeared to be streambred. Kevin Wnuck was right, this lower end of the Musconetcong River did hold plenty of cold water and trout—many of them streambred.

You'll find some great hatches on the "Musky" throughout the season. It holds plenty of caddis, including a great tan caddis hatch in May. Joe Petrella of Basking Ridge considers the Musconetcong his home stream. He's fished over many hatches in his years there, and he believes the tan caddis to be one of the best. He's also fished over trout rising to blue quills, quill gordons, and green caddis. Joe prefers matching the hatch in the Stephens State Park area, just upriver from Hackettstown. Robert Patten likes to fly-fish the area just below the park. He hikes into some of the more remote areas of the Musconetcong.

Even in late season you'll find some hatches. Justin Allsopp of Hackettstown also fishes the river frequently and has seen whiteflies on the Musconetcong in early September. Salem Towne of nearby Asbury and Ken Fischer of Milford often fly-fish the lower end of the river. Both anglers have experienced hatches on the Musconetcong.

Upriver from NJ 31 you'll find more open water. In Hampton there's some open water at the Hampton Borough Park. In the lower section, the river ranges from 50 to 60 feet wide, but in its upper section, near Hackettstown, it narrows to 40 to 50 feet. Near Hackettstown you'll also find a 1-mile no-kill stretch. NJ 57 parallels much of the river from Penwell to Hackettstown; you'll find access areas with parking along the river's lower end.

BEST TIMES TO FLY-FISH

February 1–March 31
Early black stonefly: afternoon, size 14 or 16

April 1–May 1
Little blue-winged olive dun: afternoon, size 20
Blue quill: afternoon, size 18
Quill gordon: afternoon, size 14
Grannom: afternoon, size 16
Hendrickson: afternoon, size 14
Tan caddis: afternoon, sizes 16–24

May 2–June 15
Green caddis: evening, size 16
Sulphur: evening, size 16
Dark green drake: afternoon and evening, size 8
Tan caddis: evening, size 16
Light cahill: evening, size 14
Slate drake: evening, size 12

June 16–July 31
Trico: morning, size 24

August 1–October 31
Slate drake: evening, size 14
Whitefly: evening, size 14
October caddis: afternoon, size 12

44. SOUTH BRANCH RARITAN RIVER

Fly-Fishing Only—2.5 miles in the Ken Lockwood Gorge

Year-Round Conservation Area—1.1 miles of the Claremont stretch

Rating: 7   DeLorme map: 69

Positives: *Some good hatches • Some streambred trout • Spectacular scenery in Ken Lockwood Gorge • Good deep pools and pocket water*
Negatives: *Lots of private water • Crowded conditions • Needs more signs to indicate open water*

Kevin Wnuck and I spent an entire day exploring the South Branch of the Raritan River. We drove to the headwaters near Budd Lake then downriver to Neshanic Station—that's a total of about 35 miles of stocked water.

We stopped in Long Valley at the upper end of the river and saw a decent hatch of hendricksons appear in the afternoon. The Claremont stretch in this area even holds a good number of native brook trout. This section shows what can happen when sportsmen cooperate in a goal beneficial for all. Several years ago the very active chapters of Trout Unlimited in New Jersey, along with the New Jersey Federation of Sportsmen, formed a group called the South Branch Project. Participating TU chapters included Hacklebarney, North Jersey, Central Jersey, and Ken Lockwood. This group convinced the county to purchase a 1.2-mile parcel of land where a developer planned a community, and they persuaded the state to place special regulations on the water. Currently anglers are allowed one trout more than 15 inches long, caught on artificial lures only. When groups combine for a common good, great things can happen, even in a highly industrialized state.

Kevin kept the best and the most spectacular part of the river for last. We headed down Hunterdon County Route (CR) 513 between the towns of Califon and High Bridge, turned right onto Cregar Road (which soon turned into Cokesbury Road), and headed down the hill. As soon as we crossed the bridge over the South Branch, Kevin turned left and we headed into a section of the river called the Ken Lockwood Gorge. As Kevin excitedly drove along a narrow lane, he extolled the virtues of this trout river almost lost in time. The road soon turned into a cramped, rutted dirt road designed for just one car. Paralleling the road to the west flowed a beautiful, boulder-strewn, 60-foot-wide river. At my first glance at the Ken Lockwood Gorge, I felt certain we had somehow taken a wrong turn or two and ended up on the Rapidan River in Virginia, or even Montana's

Gallatin. We traveled a mile more on the treacherous road and found much of the lower end of the gorge teeming with fly-fishers anxious to rid themselves of any thought of the just-departed winter. Kevin and I stopped about halfway up the 2-mile rutted road, assembled our gear, and began casting into some promising pocket water. In the high water that late-April afternoon, Kevin caught a couple of trout.

Not until the following August did I return to the South Branch and the Ken Lockwood Gorge, this time with my son-in-law, Rick Nowaczek. This stream and this place had haunted me. What was a dynamic river like this doing just 40 air miles from New York City? I wanted to fly-fish this intriguing water again and again. Still, I arrived there after 5 days of mid-80s temperatures, and I didn't expect to see any hatches or rising trout. Then I arrived at streamside and immediately checked the water temperature—66 degrees. The stream ran fairly full for August because of a generous supply of rain during the summer.

Rick and I headed for a midpoint in the gorge that Sunday evening at 6:30. You'll find the gorge extremely busy and crowded on weekends—it's best to fly-fish this section on a weekday. As I scanned the surface, I noted a couple of large maroon spinners already laying eggs. Several slate drake duns then took off from some fast water in the center of the stream. These large mayflies didn't crawl onto an exposed rock to emerge (like

Kevin Wnuck fishes in the Ken Lockwood Gorge.

they do on many streams), but emerged right in the water. I tied on a tandem of a Slate Drake dry fly with an *Isonychia* behind it to imitate the natural. I first cast the pair into one of the heavy riffles so common in the gorge. It led into a deep pool below. On my second cast, a large rainbow sucked in the nymph and broke off almost immediately. In the next half hour, six trout took that Slate Drake, but I didn't land one of them.

I sat back and watched Rick land a heavy rainbow upriver on a size-12 Patriot. Meanwhile, in front of me, I began seeing dozens of slate drakes emerging. Joining them were a smaller size-18 or -20 pale evening dun and a size-14 light yellow stonefly, but in fewer numbers. As I looked up to the treetops, I saw dozens of huge *Hexagenia* spinners in their characteristic undulating flight. These large, burrowing mayflies usually appear around mid-August. Here, in the middle of New Jersey, I saw all these aquatic insects appear, and I experienced one of my best August evenings of fishing ever. I began casting my Slate Drake to the head of a deep pool; a heavy holdover brown trout sucked in the pattern and went deep to sulk. I finally landed the 15-incher and started casting to another likely section of the riffle. A rainbow hit this time, and I landed and released it. Rick and I ended the evening hooking a dozen trout and missing many more.

I couldn't wait to return to the river—and I did the very next day. John Ruland, a rod builder who fishes the South Branch frequently, met me at the upper end of the gorge. A fine drizzle was falling as we parked our cars along the narrow road. By the time we entered the stream, John and I saw hundreds of little blue-wings emerging. It happens almost every time—show me some inclement weather, and I'll show you a hatch of little blue-winged olives. I tied on a size-16 Bead Head Pheasant Tail behind a Patriot dry fly. Why? The Pheasant Tail closely copies the *Baetis* nymph that was emerging that afternoon. We had only a couple of hours to fish, but we landed a half-dozen trout on that Bead Head. In 2 days of fishing on the South Branch—in the middle of August—I caught more than 20 trout. That's not bad for any river in August.

The South Branch holds a tremendous number of hatches. Recently Kevin Wnuck told me about the whitefly hatch reports on the river. Several fly-fishers told him that the whitefly appeared in early September. You'll find few anglers on the Ken Lockwood Gorge section that time of year, so you might want to give that evening hatch a try. Mark Dettmar often fishes the lower end of the South Branch near Stanton Station. He often sees heavy caddisfly hatches in May and June there.

My questions about the South Branch of the Raritan had been resoundingly answered. Did it hold trout throughout the summer? You bet it did!

Would you find any late-season hatches there? You bet you would! Is it a great trout river? You bet it is!

BEST TIMES TO FLY-FISH

February 1–March 31
Early black stonefly: afternoon, size 14 or 16

April 10–May 10
Hendrickson: afternoon, size 14
Blue quill: afternoon, size 18

May 11–June 15
Sulphur: evening, size 16
Light cahill: evening, size 14
March brown/gray fox: afternoon, size 12
Slate drake: evening, size 12
Blue-winged olive dun: afternoon, size 14
Little yellow stonefly: evening, size 16
Tan caddis: evening, size 14
Olive caddis: evening, size 16

June 16–July 31
Brown caddis: evening, size 14
Yellow drake: evening, size 10
Slate drake: evening, size 12
Little blue-winged olive dun: afternoon, size 20

August 1–September 30
Slate drake: afternoon and evening, size 12
Big slate drake *(Hexagenia)*: evening, size 8
Little blue-winged olive dun: afternoon, size 20–24
Light yellow stonefly: evening, size 14
Pale evening dun: evening, size 20
Whitefly: evening, size 14

VIII.

Patterns for the Overlooked Streams

About six years ago I began using a tandem on eastern streams. (I wrote extensively about this use of two flies in *Patterns, Hatches, Tactics, and Trout**.) Angling friends like Craig Josephson, Bob Budd, Ken Rictor, Bruce Matolyak, and my son, Bryan Meck, also found it extremely productive. On the trips to streams and rivers included in this book, we found that a tandem made up of a Patriot dry fly and a Bead Head Pheasant Tail Nymph really worked when no hatch appeared. On New Jersey's South Branch of the Raritan I caught trout on both the wet and the dry flies. On the East and West Branches of Owego Creek Craig Josephson caught trout on both the Patriot and the Bead Head—and plenty of them. Bryan Meck did rather well on the two patterns on the East Branch of Antietam Creek. If no hatch appears on your stream, try using the tandem. I've included these patterns in this chapter; see pages 183 and 184.

I recently traveled to Ontario's Grand River, where the rules say that you can use only a single barbless hook on certain areas. I used a size-16 Bead Head with a strike indicator and I had a devil of a time hooking trout. I'm convinced that they felt the weight of the indicator and let go quickly. Not so with the tandem. Trout don't feel the dry fly when they pull the wet fly below it. Very seldom do I miss a trout with the two flies.

In *Patterns, Hatches, Tactics, and Trout**, I devoted a chapter to the tandem. I showed how to connect the two patterns and how to cast them. You'll find the information in there useful if you plan to use the two patterns.

*Vivid Publishing, Inc., PO Box 1572, Williamsport, PA 17701.

If you still don't think that using a tandem really works, you've got to read this letter from Pete Ryan, by day a dentist in Coudersport, Pennsylvania.

I'm writing to share with you a couple fishing experiences I had this past week! I received your new book [Patterns, Hatches, Tactics, and Trout] a week ago Thursday and read most of it that afternoon and evening. I was of course interested in the tandem—Patriot and Green Weenie—and even dug an article out of my collection of Pennsylvania Angler articles I have kept for "future reference." (My wife says I save too much junk—but one never knows!) Anyway, while watching football games on Sunday, I tied a dozen Patriots and weighted Weenies. I intended to fish Labor Day morning on the "no-kill" stretch of the Genesee River east of Wellsville, New York, just 30 minutes over the mountain from my house. The Genesee holds more water than the other watersheds around here, and after the drought conditions we've had, I hoped to find enough water in which to fish. I left my house determined to try the tandem and took only those flies plus a box of Tricos and Midges—just in case.

I arrived in the parking area at 9:30 only to meet Bryan Kehoe, one of my fishing buddies, leaving the stream. He was disgusted—having fished for 3 hours and no trout. I explained to him what I intended to do and showed him the two flies. He laughed and tried to talk me into going to the Oswayo, but I was determined to give the tandem a chance. So as Bryan watched from his car, I caught two nice browns on my first five casts in the first run! He yelled an obscenity at me and drove away! I quit fishing at 12:30 after an additional 12 trout—all on the Green Weenie. Not bad, 14 trout in 3 hours on a heavily fished, no-kill stream with no surface activity, no hatches, and drought conditions. I never changed my original tandem setup and even got home in time to mow my lawn with a smile on my face!

Last Wednesday night, Stew Dickerson, with whom you fished the Oswayo a few years back, gave me a call and said he had done really well fishing tricos and ants on the Genesee in Scio, New York, about 6 miles downstream from Wellsville. Stew knows I love fishing small flies on fine tippets to rising fish, so of course I jumped at the chance. The next morning the water, as expected, was extremely low, but there were five deep runs in a half-mile stretch that Stew promised held fish. Tricos were dancing in the air when we hit the stream at 8 AM. Stew caught two trout on an ant, and I could only manage a few smallmouth bass fishing a midge in the first run. We worked our way upstream fishing ants, beetles, midges, and trico spinners, and by 10 o'clock I had managed to catch two trout and Stew also had a few more.

Stew started to apologize for our lack of success after his glowing promise of great fishing. I told Stew to relax—I was about to give the tandem another try! Three casts into a run that I had pounded for 25 minutes produced two trout. In 5 minutes I had five trout. Stew begged a Patriot and a Green Weenie off me and we proceeded to work our way back downstream to our car. Between us, we caught 31 trout in the next 2 hours, all on the Green Weenie, except for one 17½-inch brown that blasted my Patriot as it danced in a riffle at the head of a deep run.

I have also fished a tandem on the Big Horn, but had never given thought to trying it here at home. Just want to thank you for sharing your expertise with those of us who aren't as fortunate to fish as often as you are able! My only concern is that the tandem may take the excitement and pleasure out of fooling fish—but I doubt it.

Does the tandem setup work? You better believe it does! Does the Green Weenie work on the streams in the Northeast? It certainly does!

Do you prefer to use just a dry fly when no hatch appears? Ask Diane Budd of Hollidaysburg, Pennsylvania, what her favorite dry-fly pattern is. You'll find Diane using the Patriot, almost exclusively, throughout the entire season.

I've used another extremely productive pattern on my trips to the overlooked trout streams: I call it the Bead Head Olive Caddis. This pattern, along with the Patriot dry fly and the Bead Head Pheasant Tail Nymph—and, of course, the Green Weenie—make up the four patterns I always have with me. For most nonhatch days these patterns should work well for you.

But on many of the streams we've included in this book you'll find hatches—on some of them you'll find great hatches. For these, try the patterns in this chapter.

Patterns to Use
When There's No Hatch to Match

Patriot
Thread: Red
Tails: Brown hackle fibers
Body: Smolt blue Krystal Flash wound around the shank. Wind some of the red thread in the middle of the shank, similar to the Royal Coachman.
Wings: White impala or calf tail, divided
Hackle: Brown
Hook: Mustad 94833, size 10–18

The ever-popular Patriot dry fly

The Bead Head Pheasant Tail Nymph

The Green Weenie

BEAD HEAD PHEASANT TAIL NYMPH
Thread: Dark brown
Tail: Five or six fibers from a ring-neck pheasant tail
Body: Continue winding the pheasant tail fibers used to tie in the tail up to the bead, and tie in
Thorax: Copper bead
Hackle: Ten pheasant tail fibers
Hook: Tiemco 2457, size 12–16

GREEN WEENIE
Body: Cut off a 5-inch piece of small or medium chartreuse chenille. Form a small loop with the chenille extending out over the bend of the hook, then wrap the chenille around the shank of the hook up to the eye.
Hook: Mustad 9672, size 10 or 12
Tying Notes: I include a loop as the tail of the Green Weenie. I feel this loop makes the pattern move as it drifts downstream. I often add weight to the body. I add 10, 15, 20, and 25 wraps of .015 lead, then color code the patterns. For 25 wraps I use orange thread, for 20 wraps I use a chartreuse thread, etc.

A Bead Head Olive Caddis works especially well on limestone streams.

BEAD HEAD OLIVE CADDIS
Thread: Olive
Head: Copper bead
Body: Dubbed with a heavy amount of dark olive opossum fur, ribbed with fine gold wire
Hook: Tiemco 2457, size 12–16

Patterns That Match the Hatches

Note: If you plan to tie the dun pattern as a dry fly, use the Mustad 94840 hook listed. If you want to tie a wet fly to copy the dun, then use the Mustad 3906. You'll see both hook numbers listed under many of the following dun recipes.

Mayfly Imitations

BLUE DUN OR LITTLE BLUE-WINGED OLIVE DUN

Copies *Baetis tricaudatus* and other *Baetis* species

Thread: Dark gray

Tail: Medium to dark gray hackle fibers

Body: Gray muskrat or medium gray poly, dubbed; for the Little Blue-Winged Olive, use olive-gray poly

Wings: On smaller sizes (20), use dark gray mallard quills; on larger sizes, use dark gray hackle tips; for the tandem, use a dark gray deer hair wing and tie the pattern as a parachute dry fly

Hackle: Blue dun

Hook: Mustad 94840, size 18 or 20

RUSTY SPINNER

Thread: Dark brown

Tail: Dark grayish brown hackle fibers

Body: Grayish brown poly, dubbed and ribbed with fine tan thread

Wings: Pale gray poly yarn, tied spent

Hook: Mustad 94833, size 18 or 20

BAETIS NYMPH

Thread: Dark olive

Tail: Wood duck fibers, dyed dark olive

Body: Dark olive-brown opossum

Wings: Dark gray mallard quill section

Hackle: Cree or ginger variant, dyed dark olive

Hook: Mustad 3906B, size 18

BAETIS EMERGER

Thread: Dark olive

Tail: Dark brownish olive hackle fibers

Body: Dark grayish olive muskrat, dubbed

Thorax: Dark gray poly yarn tied over top of muskrat

Throat: Dark brown grouse hackle fibers

Hook: Mustad 3906B or 94840, size 20

A Blue Quill works well when Paraleptophlebia *species emerge.*

BLUE QUILL

Copies most *Paraleptophlebia* species

Thread: Dark gray

Tail: Medium to dark gray hackle fibers

Body: Eyed peacock herl, stripped or dark gray poly, dubbed

Wings: Dark gray hackle tips
Hackle: Light to medium blue dun
Hook: Mustad 94840 or 3906, size
18 or 20

DARK BROWN SPINNER
Thread: Dark brown
Tail: Dark brown hackle fibers
Body: Dark brown poly, dubbed
Wings: Pale gray poly yarn, tied spent
Hook: Mustad 94840, size 18 or 20

PARA NYMPH
Thread: Dark brown
Tail: Mallard flank feather, dyed dark
brown
Body: Dark brown angora, dubbed
Wings: One dark gray mallard quill,
tied down
Hackle: Dark gray
Hook: Mustad 3906B, size 16 or 18

PARA EMERGER
Thread: Dark brown
Tail: Dark brown hackle fibers
Body: Dark grayish brown angora,
dubbed
Thorax: Gray poly yarn pulled over
top of dubbed brown angora
Throat: Dark brown hackle fibers
Hook: Mustad 3906B or 94840, size
16 or 18

QUILL GORDON
Copies species like *Epeorus pleuralis*
Thread: Dark gray
Tail: Dark gray hackle fibers
Body: Eyed peacock herl, stripped and
lacquered
Wings: Wood duck or imitation wood
duck, divided; or dark gray hackle
tips
Hackle: Dark gray
Hook: Mustad 94840 or 3906,
size 14

QUILL GORDON NYMPH
Thread: Dark brown
Tail: Fibers from a mallard flank
feather, dyed dark amber
Body: Dark brown fur or angora,
mixed with a bit of lighter brown
or amber
Wings: Mottled brown turkey, tied
down over thorax
Hackle: Cree or ginger variant (dark
and amber mixed)
Hook: Mustad 3906B, size 14

QUILL GORDON EMERGER
Thread: Tannish brown
Tail: Brown mallard flank
Body: Tannish brown angora; dark
gray turkey folded back over body
like a wet fly
Hackle: Grouse
Hook: Mustad 3906B or 94840, size 14

A Hendrickson tied parachute-style

RED QUILL AND HENDRICKSON
The Red Quill copies the male and the
Hendrickson the female of
Ephemerella subvaria and several
closely related subspecies. In
addition, the Red Quill effectively
imitates many spinners like
*Ephemerella subvaria, Epeorus
pleuralis,* and the male spinner of
Ephemerella invaria and *E.
rotunda.*

Thread: Brown
Tail: Medium gray hackle fibers
Body: Red Quill: reddish brown hackle fiber stripped of its barbules and wound from the bend of the hook to the wings. Hendrickson: tan poly, dubbed.
Wings: Wood duck, divided. Optional on Hendrickson are gray hackle tips.
Hackle: Medium gray
Hook: Mustad 94840 or 3906, size 14 or 16

RED QUILL SPINNER
Thread: Brown
Tail: Bronze dun hackle fibers
Body: Dark tannish brown poly, dubbed and ribbed finely with tan thread
Wings: Pale gray poly yarn, tied spent
Hook: Mustad 94840, size 14 or 16

HENDRICKSON NYMPH
Thread: Dark brown
Tail: Dark ginger hackle fibers
Body: Black angora, dubbed
Wings: Mottled brown turkey, tied down over thorax
Hackle: Ginger
Hook: Mustad 3906B, size 12 or 14

A Hendrickson Emerger

HENDRICKSON EMERGER
Thread: Tan
Tail: Tan grouse
Body: Brownish black angora
Thorax: Dark gray turkey

Throat: Tan grouse
Hook: Mustad 3906B or 9671, size 14

DARK QUILL GORDON
Copies species like *Ameletus ludens*
Thread: Black
Tail: Very dark dun
Body: Very dark gray poly, ribbed with lighter gray thread
Wings: Dark gray hackle tips
Hackle: Dark dun
Hook: Mustad 94840, size 14

DARK QUILL GORDON SPINNER
Thread: Black
Tail: Dark gray
Body: Same as dun
Wings: Pale gray poly yarn, tied spent
Hook: Mustad 94840, size 14

GREAT SPECKLED OLIVE DUN
Copies mayflies like *Siphloplecton basale*
Thread: Pale gray
Tail: Medium blue dun fibers
Body: Pale gray poly, dubbed
Wings: Mallard flank
Hackle: Medium blue dun
Hook: Mustad 94840, size 12

GREAT SPECKLED SPINNER
Thread: Pale gray
Tail: Bronze dun variant fibers
Body: Pale gray poly, dubbed
Wings: Pale tan poly yarn
Hackle: Bronze dun variant
Hook: Mustad 94840, size 12

BLACK QUILL
Copies *Leptophlebia cupida*
Thread: Dark brown
Tail: Dark bronze dun hackle fibers
Body: Eyed peacock herl, stripped
Wings: Dark gray hackle tips
Hackle: Dark brown with a turn or two of tan in the rear
Hook: Mustad 94840, size 14

Early Brown Spinner

Thread: Dark brown
Tail: Dark brown hackle fibers
Body: Dark reddish brown polypropylene ribbed with pale yellow thread
Wings: Pale tan polypropylene
Hackle: Dark brown
Hook: Mustad 94840, size 14

Black Quill Nymph

Thread: Dark brown
Tail: Dark brown hackle fibers
Body: Chocolate brown angora, loosely dubbed
Wings: Dark mallard section
Hackle: Dark brown
Hook: Mustad 3906B or 9671, size 12 or 14

Black Quill Emerger

Thread: Dark brown
Tail: Dark brown hackle fibers
Body: Dark brown rabbit
Wings: Dark gray poly yarn
Hackle: Dark grouse
Hook: Mustad 3906B, size 14

Sulphur Dun

Copies *Ephemerella rotunda, E. invaria, E. septentrionalis,* and, to a lesser degree, *E. dorothea*
Thread: Yellow
Tail: Cream hackle fibers
Body: Usually pale yellow poly with an orange (and sometimes olive-orange) cast (for *E. dorothea,* use pale yellow poly)
Wings: Pale gray hackle tips
Hackle: Cream
Hook: Mustad 94840 or 3906, size 16 or 18

Sulphur Spinner

Thread: Tan
Tail: Tan deer hair
Body: Female with eggs: yellowish tan poly; female without eggs: tan poly; male: bright red hackle stem, stripped and wound around hook
Wings: Pale gray poly yarn, tied spent (also tie some upright)
Hook: Mustad 94840, size 16 or 18

Sulphur Nymph

Thread: Grayish brown
Tail: Brown pheasant tail fibers
Body: Brown (ground color) fur
Wings: Dark gray mallard quill section, tied down over thorax
Hackle: Cree
Hook: Mustad 3906B, size 14–18

Sulphur Emerger

Thread: Tan
Tail: Dark brown grouse hackle fibers
Body: Pale tan angora, dubbed
Thorax: A short pale gray turkey feather
Throat: Dark brown grouse fibers
Hook: Mustad 3906B or 94840, size 14 or 16

Little Blue Dun

Copies many *Baetis* species (especially those formally classified as *Pseudocloeon*)
Thread: Gray
Tail: Medium dun hackle fibers
Body: Dark gray poly, dubbed
Wings: Dark gray hackle tips
Hackle: Dark gray
Hook: Mustad 94840, size 20 or 22

Rusty Spinner

Thread: Dark brown
Tail: Dark brown hackle fibers
Body: Dark brown poly, dubbed
Wings: Pale gray poly yarn, tied spent
Hook: Mustad 94840, size 20 or 22

Pale Evening Dun

Copies species like *Heptagenia aphrodite, H. hebe,* and *Ephemerella dorothea*
Thread: Pale yellow
Tail: Creamish yellow hackle fibers
Body: Creamish yellow poly with olive cast (*H. hebe* has no olive cast)
Wings: Pale gray mallard flank
Hackle: Yellowish cream
Hook: Mustad 94840, size 16

Pale Evening Spinner

Thread: Pale yellow
Tail: Cream hackle fibers
Body: Pale yellow poly
Wings: White poly tied spent
Hackle: Pale yellow
Hook: Mustad 94840, size 16

Gray Fox

Copies *Stenonema fuscum* (many entomologists now list this with *Stenonema vicarium*—the March brown)
Thread: Cream
Tail: Tan deer hair
Body: Cream poly, dubbed
Wings: Mallard flank feather, dyed pale yellowish tan, divided
Hackle: Cree, or one brown and one cream mixed
Hook: Mustad 94840 or 3906, size 12 or 14

Ginger Quill Spinner

Thread: Brown
Tail: Dark brown hackle fibers
Body: Eyed peacock herl, dyed tan and stripped, or grayish brown poly, ribbed with brown thread
Wings: Gray hackle tips (conventional); or pale gray poly yarn, tied spent

Hackle: Dark ginger (conventional); or none with poly yarn wings
Hook: Mustad 94840, size 12 or 14

Gray Fox Nymph

Thread: Brown
Tail: Fibers from a mallard flank feather, dyed brown
Body: Brown angora yarn, tied on top over cream. Tie in brown at tail, and dub in cream so that top (tergite) of body is brown and the belly (sternite) is cream.
Wings: Dark brown turkey, tied down over thorax
Hackle: Dark cree
Hook: Mustad 3906B, size 12

Gray Fox Emerger

Thread: Brown
Tail: Dark grouse
Body: Pale tan angora
Thorax: Pale gray turkey
Throat: Dark grouse
Hook: Mustad 3906B or 94840, size 12 or 14

March Brown

Copies *Stenonema vicarium*
Thread: Yellow
Tail: Dark brown hackle fibers
Body: Tan poly, dubbed and ribbed with dark brown thread
Wings: Mallard flank feather, dyed yellowish brown and divided
Hackle: One cream and one dark brown, mixed
Hook: Mustad 94840 or 3906, size 12

Great Red Spinner

Thread: Dark brown
Tail: Dark brown hackle fibers
Body: Dark reddish brown poly, dubbed
Wings: Pale gray poly yarn, tied spent

Hackle: Dark brown with a turn or two of pale ginger mixed
Hook: Mustad 94840, size 12

MARCH BROWN NYMPH
Thread: Brown
Tail: Fibers from a mallard flank feather, dyed brown
Body: Cream poly, dubbed
Wings: Dark brown turkey, tied down over thorax
Hackle: Dark cree
Hook: Mustad 3906B, size 12

MARCH BROWN EMERGER
Thread: Brown
Tail: Grouse
Body: Cream angora
Wings: Brown
Hackle: Brown grouse
Hook: Mustad 3906B or 94840, size 12

A Light Cahill tied parachute-style

LIGHT CAHILL
Copies *Stenacron interpunctatum* and many *Stenonema* species like *S. ithaca*
Thread: Cream
Tail: Cream hackle fibers
Body: Creamish yellow poly (for the female *interpunctatum,* use pale orange poly)
Wings: Mallard flank feather, dyed pale yellow, divided

Hackle: Cree
Hook: Mustad 94840 or 3906, size 14

LIGHT CAHILL SPINNER
Same as Light Cahill (above), except omit hackle and add pale yellow poly yarn for wings. Tie them spent.

LIGHT CAHILL NYMPH
Thread: Brown
Tail: Fibers from a mallard flank feather, dyed brown
Body: Dark brown angora yarn on top and pale amber belly, dubbed
Wings: Dark brown turkey
Hackle: Dark cree
Hook: Mustad 3906B, size 12

LIGHT CAHILL EMERGER
Thread: Tan
Tail: Dark grouse
Body: Tan angora
Wings: Pale gray turkey
Hackle: Light grouse
Hook: Mustad 3906B, size 14

SLATE DRAKE
Copies many *Isonychia* species
Thread: Black
Tail: Dark gray hackle fibers
Body: Peacock herl (not from eye), stripped; or dark gray poly; or muskrat, dubbed
Wings: Dark gray hackle tips
Hackle: One cream hackle tied in behind and one dark brown hackle tied in front
Hook: Mustad 94840 or 3906, size 12 or 14

WHITE-GLOVED HOWDY
Thread: Dark brown or maroon
Tail: Medium gray hackle fibers
Body: Dark mahogany poly, dubbed
Wings: Pale gray poly yarn
Hook: Mustad 94840, size 14

ISONYCHIA EMERGER
Thread: Black
Tail: Black
Body: Brownish black angora
Wings: Black turkey
Hackle: Dark gray fibers
Hook: Mustad 3906B, size 14

ISONYCHIA NYMPH
Thread: Dark brown
Tail: Three dark brown hackles with one side cut off
Body: Very dark brown angora or opossum
Wings: Dark gray mallard quill section, tied down over thorax
Hackle: Cree, dyed pale olive
Hook: Mustad 3906B, size 10 or 12

BROWN DRAKE
Copies mayflies like *Ephemera simulans*
Thread: Brown
Tail: Dark brown deer hair
Body: Grayish tan poly
Wings: Grayish tan flank feather
Hackle: Dark brown with a few turns of ginger
Hook: Mustad 94831, size 14

BROWN DRAKE SPINNER
Thread: Brown
Tail: Dark brown deer hair
Body: Dark tannish yellow poly with dark brown markings
Wings: Pale tan poly yarn with dark brown fibers tied upright or spent
Hackle: Dark brown with a few turns of ginger
Hook: Mustad 94831, size 14

BROWN DRAKE NYMPH
Thread: Brown
Tail: Three light brown hackles, trimmed and tied in
Body: Pale tan angora or opossum

Wings: Brown turkey, tied down and over thorax
Hackle: Dark cree
Hook: Mustad 3906B or 9672, size 10 or 12

BROWN DRAKE EMERGER
Thread: Brown
Tail: Light brown
Body: Tan angora
Wings: Tan turkey
Hackle: Grouse
Hook: Mustad 3906B or 94840, size 12

GRAY DRAKE
Copies *Siphlonurus quebecensis*
Thread: Black
Tail: Dark dun
Body: Dark gray poly
Wings: Dark gray hackle tips or dark gray deer hair
Legs: Dark dun
Hook: Mustad 94840, size 12

GRAY DRAKE SPINNER
Thread: Black
Tail: Dark gray hackle fibers
Body: Black poly ribbed with a pale gray thread
Wings: White poly, tied spent
Hook: Mustad 94840, size 12

PINK LADY OR PINK CAHILL
Copies the female of *Epeorus vitreus*
Thread: Cream
Tail: Dark blue dun hackle fibers
Body: Male: pale yellow; female: pinkish cream poly
Wings: Pale yellow mallard flank
Hackle: Creamish yellow
Hook: Mustad 94840, size 14

SALMON SPINNER
Thread: Salmon
Tail: Cream ginger hackle fibers
Body: Coral polypropylene

Wings: Pale gray polypropylene
Hackle: Cream ginger
Hook: Mustad 94840, size 14

VITREUS NYMPH
Thread: Tan
Tail: Dark brown fibers from a
   pheasant tail
Body: Dub amber on the entire body.
   Bring the butts of the pheasant tail
   up and over the body, and tie in
   where you tie in the wings.
Wings: Brown turkey section
Hackle: Several turns of ginger
Hook: Mustad 3906B, size 14

BLUE-WINGED OLIVE DUN
Copies many *Drunella* and *Dannella*
   species like *Drunella cornuta,*
   Drunella longicornus, Drunella
   cornutella, and *Drunella lata*
Thread: Olive
Tail: Grayish olive hackle fibers
Body: Light to medium olive poly,
   dubbed
Wings: Dark gray hackle tips
Hackle: Medium creamish olive
Hook: Mustad 94840 or 3906, size
   14–20

DARK OLIVE SPINNER
Thread: Dark olive or black
Tail: Moose mane (dark brown)
Body: Dark olive poly (almost black
   with an olive cast)
Wings: Pale gray poly yarn, tied spent
Hook: Mustad 94840, size 14–20

DRUNELLA NYMPH
Thread: Olive
Tail: Wood duck
Body: Dark brown angora tied over
   dubbed-in olive opossum
Wings: Brown turkey
Hackle: Ginger variant, dyed olive
Hook: Mustad 3906B, size 14–18

DRUNELLA EMERGER
Thread: Olive
Tail: Olive wood duck
Body: Olive angora
Wings: Gray turkey
Hackle: Dark grouse
Hook: Mustad 3906B, size 14–18

The Green Drake works well on New York and Pennsylvania streams that hold hatches of the naturals.

GREEN DRAKE
Copies *Ephemera guttulata*
Thread: Cream
Tail: Moose mane
Body: Cream poly, dubbed
Wings: Mallard flank dyed yellowish
   green, divided
Hackle: Rear: cream; front: dark
   brown
Hook: Mustad 94831 or 3906B, size
   8 or 10

COFFIN FLY
Thread: White
Tail: Light tan deer hair
Body: White poly, dubbed
Wings: Grayish yellow poly yarn, tied
   spent
Hook: Mustad 94831, size 8 or 10

GREEN DRAKE NYMPH
Thread: Tan
Tail: Three medium brown hackles,
   trimmed and tied in

Body: Pale tan angora
Wings: Dark brown turkey, tied down
   and over thorax
Hackle: Cree
Hook: Mustad 3906B or 9672, size
   8–12

Green Drake Emerger
Thread: Tan
Tail: Grouse
Body: Tan angora
Wings: Pale yellow poly yarn
Hackle: Light grouse
Hook: Mustad 3906B or 94840, size
   8–12

Chocolate Dun
Copies species like *Eurylophella
   (Ephemerella) bicolor* and
   Ephemerella needhami
Thread: Brown
Tail: Medium gray
Body: Chocolate brown poly finely
   ribbed with lighter brown thread
Wings: Dark gray hackle tips
Hackle: Tan
Hook: Mustad 94840 or 3906, size 16

Chocolate Spinner
Thread: Dark brown
Tail: Tannish gray hackle fibers
Body: Dark rusty brown poly, dubbed
Wings: Pale gray poly yarn, tied spent
Hook: Mustad 94840, size 16

Chocolate Dun Nymph
Thread: Brown
Tail: Light brown mallard flank
   feather fibers
Body: Light brown poly nymph
   dubbing
Wings: Dark gray mallard quill
Hackle: Brown
Hook: Mustad 3906B, size 16

Chocolate Dun Emerger
Thread: Brown
Tail: Light brown grouse
Body: Brown angora
Wings: Gray poly
Hackle: Brown grouse
Hook: Mustad 3906B or 94840,
   size 16

Dark Green Drake
Copies species like *Litobrancha
   recurvata*
Thread: Dark gray
Tail: Dark brown moose mane
Body: Very dark slate poly, dubbed
   and ribbed with yellow thread
Wings: Mallard flank, heavily barred
   and dyed dark green
Hackle: Rear: tannish brown; front:
   dark brown
Hook: Mustad 94833 or 3906B, size
   8 or 10

Brown Drake Spinner
Thread: Brown
Tail: Brown hackle fibers
Body: Reddish brown poly, dubbed
   and ribbed with yellow thread
Wings: Pale gray poly yarn, tied spent
Hackle: Dark brown
Hook: Mustad 94833, size 8 or 10

Dark Green Drake Nymph
Thread: Light brown
Tail: Three dark bronze hackles,
   trimmed and tied in
Body: Tan with a grayish cast angora,
   or opossum
Wings: Dark brown turkey
Hackle: Dark cree
Hook: Mustad 9672, size 8 or 10

Dark Green Drake Emerger
Thread: Tan
Tail: Brown grouse

Body: Medium tan angora
Wings: Poly
Hackle: Light grouse
Hook: Mustad 9672 or 94840, size 8 or 10

BLUE-WINGED OLIVE DUN

Copies species like *Attenella (Ephemerella) attenuata*
Thread: Olive
Tail: Blue dun hackle fibers
Body: Medium olive hackle stem or muskrat, dyed olive
Wings: Dark bluish gray
Hackle: Medium olive
Hook: Mustad 94840, size 14

DARK OLIVE SPINNER

Thread: Dark brown
Tail: Blue dun hackle fibers
Body: Dark brown fur with an olive cast
Wings: Pale gray hackle tips
Hackle: Blue dun hackle
Hook: Mustad 94840, size 14

CREAM CAHILL

Copies species like *Stenonema pulchellum* and *S. modestum*
Thread: Cream
Tail: Tan hackle fibers
Body: White or pale cream polypropylene
Wings: Very pale cream mallard flank feather
Hackle: Cream
Hook: Mustad 94840, size 14 or 16

CREAM CAHILL SPINNER

Thread: Pale yellow
Tail: Pale tan hackle fibers
Body: White poly (pale cream body)
Wing: Pale gray poly yarn
Hackle: Pale cream
Hook: Mustad 94840, size 14 or 16

CREAM CAHILL NYMPH

Thread: Olive brown
Tail: Light brown hackle fibers
Body: Dub pale creamish gray on hook, then tie pale brownish olive yarn in at bend and bring over top to wing case and tie in
Wings: Dark brown turkey
Hackle: Dark olive-brown
Hook: Mustad 3906B, size 14 or 16

CREAM CAHILL EMERGER

Thread: Cream
Tail: Brown grouse
Body: Creamish tan angora
Wings: White poly
Hackle: Brown grouse
Hook: Mustad 3906B or 94840, size 14 or 16

LIGHT CAHILL

Copies species like *Heptagenia marginalis*
Thread: Cream
Tail: Dark brown hackle fibers
Body: Yellowish cream polypropylene
Wings: Yellow mallard flank
Hackle: One cream and one blue dun
Hook: Mustad 94840, size 12

OLIVE CAHILL SPINNER

Thread: Cream
Tail: Dark brown hackle fibers
Body: Fox belly fur dubbed brown
Wings: Pale gray hackle tips or cream poly yarn, tied spent
Hackle: Front: dark brown; rear: cream with darker markings
Hook: Mustad 94840, size 12

YELLOW DRAKE

Copies species like *Ephemera varia*
Thread: Pale yellow
Tail: Pale deer hair

A Yellow Drake tied parachute-style

Body: Pale yellow polypropylene
(primrose)
Wings: Pale yellow mallard flank
Hackle: Creamish yellow with a turn
of grizzly in front
Hook: Mustad 94840, size 10 or 12

YELLOW DRAKE SPINNER
Thread: Pale yellow
Tail: Dark deer hair
Body: Pale creamish yellow poly-
propylene
Wings: Mallard flank or pale poly,
tied spent
Hackle: Dun variant
Hook: Mustad 94840, size 10 or 12

YELLOW DRAKE NYMPH
Thread: Tan
Tail: Pale gray, trimmed
Body: Amber-colored angora or
opossum
Wings: Medium to light brown turkey
Hackle: Ginger
Hook: Mustad 3906B, size 10 or 12

YELLOW DRAKE EMERGER
Thread: Cream
Tail: Light grouse
Body: Pale tan angora
Wings: Pale gray poly yarn
Hackle: Light grouse
Hook: Mustad 3906B, size 12

GOLDEN DRAKE
Copies species like
Anthopotamanthus distinctus
Thread: Orange
Tail: Cream hackle fibers
Body: Yellowish orange poly
Wings: Pale gray hackle tips
Hackle: Cream
Hook: Mustad 94833, size 12 or 14

GOLDEN SPINNER
Thread: Orange
Tail: Cream hackle fibers
Body: Creamish orange
Wings: White poly yarn tied spent
Hook: Mustad 94833, size 12 or 14

BIG SLATE DRAKE
Copies large mayflies like *Hexagenia*
atrocaudata
Thread: Dark gray
Tail: Dark gray hackle fibers
Body: Peacock, stripped (take from
bottom of herl)
Wings: Dark gray calf tail
Hackle: Dark brown
Hook: Mustad 94831, size 8

DARK RUSTY SPINNER
Thread: Dark brown
Tail: Dark brown hackle fibers
Body: Tannish yellow polypropylene
ribbed with dark brown thread
Wings: Brown mallard flank feathers,
or tan poly
Hackle: One dark brown in front and
one tannish yellow in the rear
Hook: 94840, size 6

NYMPH
Thread: Amber
Tail: Olive-brown hackle fibers
Body: Tan angora, dubbed
Wings: Dark mallard quill
Hackle: Grouse
Hook: Mustad 3906B, size 6

TRICO

Copies all *Tricorythodes* species
Thread: Pale olive
Tail: Cream hackle fibers
Body: Pale olive-green poly, dubbed;
    male dun: dark brown poly
Wings: Pale gray hackle tips
Hackle: Cream
Hook: Mustad 94840, size 20–24

A female Trico Spinner

TRICO SPINNER

Thread: Dark brown
Tail: Female: short cream hackle
    fibers; male: long dark brown
    moose mane
Body: Female: rear one-third is
    cream poly, dubbed, and front
    two-thirds is dark brown poly,
    dubbed; male: dark brown poly,
    dubbed and ribbed with a very
    fine light tan thread
Wings: White poly yarn, tied spent
Hook: Mustad 94840, size 20–24

TRICO NYMPH

Thread: Black
Tail: Dark brown hackle fibers
Body: Dark brownish black fur
Wings: Dark gray mallard quill
    section
Hackle: Dark reddish brown
Hook: Mustad 3906B, size 22

WHITEFLY

Copies mayflies like the female
    Ephoron leukon
Thread: White
Tail: White hackle fibers
Body: White poly
Wings: White calf body hair
Hackle: White
Hook: Mustad 94840, size 14

WHITEFLY NYMPH

Thread: Tan
Tail: Light brown hackle fibers
Body: Pale tan
Wings: Mottled brown turkey
Hackle: Ginger
Hook: Mustad 3906B, size 12

WHITEFLY EMERGER

Thread: Tan
Tail: Light brown hackle fibers
Body: Creamish tan angora
Wings: Pale gray poly
Hackle: Ginger
Hook: Mustad 3906B or 94840, size
    12 or 14

Stonefly Imitations

Copies species like *Capnia vernalis*
    appearing in the winter

EARLY BLACK STONEFLY NYMPH

Thread: Black
Tail: Black mink fibers
Body: Black angora
Wing pad: Dark gray hackle
Hackle: Black
Hook: Mustad 3906B, size 14–18

EARLY BLACK STONEFLY ADULT

Thread: Black
Tail: Short black moose mane
Body: Black poly, dubbed
Wings: Pale gray deer hair
Hackle: Black

Hook: Mustad 94833, sizes 14–18

EARLY BROWN STONEFLY
Copies species like *Strophopteryx fasciata*
ADULT
Thread: Yellow
Tail: Short dark brown hackle fibers
Body: Dark grayish brown poly, dubbed; or peacock herl, stripped
Wings: Dark brown deer hair
Hackle: Dark brown
Hook: Mustad 94840, 3906, size 12 or 14
NYMPH
Thread: Brown
Tail: Fibers from a brown pheasant tail
Body: Reddish brown ultratranslucent dubbing
Wings: Brown turkey
Hackle: Brown
Hook: Mustad 3906B, size 12

LIGHT STONEFLY
Copies species like *Isoperla signata*
ADULT
Thread: Pale yellow
Tail: Short ginger hackle fibers
Body: Pale yellow poly, dubbed and ribbed with tan thread
Wings: Very light tan to cream deer hair
Hackle: Ginger
Hook: Mustad 94840 or 3906, size 12 or 14
NYMPH
Thread: Tan
Tail: Fibers from a mallard flank feather, dyed brown
Body: Tan fox or nymph dubbing
Wings: Light brown turkey
Hackle: Cree
Hook: Mustad 3906B, size 12

LITTLE GREEN STONEFLY
Copies species like *Alloperla imbecilla*
Thread: Green
Tail: Short pale cream hackle fibers
Body: Medium green poly, dubbed
Wings: Pale gray hackle tips, tied downwing
Hackle: Pale creamish green
Hook: Mustad 94840, size 16

YELLOW SALLY OR LITTLE YELLOW STONEFLY
Copies species like *Isoperla bilineata*
Thread: Yellow
Tail: Short cream hackle fibers
Body: Pale yellow poly, dubbed
Wings: Cream hackle tips, tied downwing
Hackle: Cree
Hook: Mustad 94840, size 14 or 16

Caddisfly Imitations

LITTLE BLACK CADDIS
Copies *Chimarra atterima*
Thread: Black
Body: Black poly, dubbed
Wings: Deer hair dyed dark gray
Hackle: Dark brown
Hook: Mustad 94840, size 16

GRANNOM
Copies many species of the genus *Brachycentrus*
Thread: Black
Body: Dark brownish black to black poly, dubbed
Wings: Dark brown deer hair
Hackle: Dark brown
Hook: Mustad 94840, size 10–16

SPOTTED SEDGE
Copies *Symphitopsyche slossanae*
Thread: Tan
Body: Tan poly, dubbed

Wings: Medium brown deer hair
Hackle: Ginger
Hook: Mustad 94840, size 14 or 16

DARK BLUE SEDGE
Copies *Psilotreta frontalis*
Thread: Dark gray
Body: Dark gray poly, dubbed
Wings: Dark grayish brown deer hair
Hackle: Dark brownish black
Hook: Mustad 94840, size 12

CREAM CADDIS
Copies some *Symphitopsyche* species
  and some *Psilotreta* species
Thread: Tan
Body: Creamish tan poly, dubbed
Wings: Medium brown deer hair
Hackle: Ginger
Hook: Mustad 94840, size 14

AUTUMN SEDGE
Copies *Neophylax* species that appear
  in the fall
Thread: Orange
Body: Tan poly with an orange cast,
  dubbed
Wings: Medium tan deer hair
Hackle: Ginger
Hook: Mustad 94840, size 10–14

IX.

Teach a Youngster Fly-Fishing and Make a Conservationist for Life

So what does teaching youngsters about fly-fishing and conservation have to do with the overlooked streams of the Northeast? On my fishing trips over the past few years, I've been impressed with the number of adults I've seen going above and beyond the call to make certain that they instill in the next generation an appreciation of the outdoors, conservation, and fly-fishing. In *Pennsylvania Trout Streams and Their Hatches,* I wrote about the splendid program that Charles McKinney and Paul Hinds developed at Baldwin High School. This project, called Family Ties, has deservedly received national attention. But as I've traveled throughout the northeastern United States and Canada lately, I've became more and more impressed with the diversity of group and individual efforts.

In many sections of the country—no, of North America—interested adults have spent substantial time teaching youngsters and young adults to fly-fish. I was fortunate enough to attend the pioneer program almost 50 years ago at Penn State University's Conservation Camp. One of the teachers who had a tremendous influence on me was George Harvey. He taught me both how to tie flies and how to fly-fish. The Conservation Camp was a total outdoor experience that has had an effect on my thinking about the environment ever since.

In the past couple of years Trout Unlimited, Family Ties, and the Fly Fishers Apprentice Program have begun programs for young adults. Efforts to teach youngsters the values of fly-fishing also reach into Canada. And we cannot forget the valuable efforts by individuals within the fly-fishing fraternity. Let's look at each in some detail.

I recently met three young men in Waterdown, Ontario, who had completed a fly-fishing program: Jamie Wilson, Matthew Kielbiski, and Michael Marozzo, who all attended the Grindstone Youth Fly Anglers Program. Conducted by John Valk and others, this program teaches stream etiquette, conservation, fly-tying, fly-fishing, and even stream entomology. I had a chance to chat with these three individuals, and if they're examples of the new blood we're getting into the sport, it bodes well for the future of fly-fishing. Michael Marozzo, by the way, won first place in the Canadian Fly Tying Classic, junior division. John Valk reports that 40 to 60 youngsters have already requested information on the next program.

Jack Beck's a dentist by day, but on weekends and evenings he devotes plenty of time to his avocation, fly-fishing. Recently Jack and Inky Moore established the Rivers Conservation and Fly Fishing Youth Camp in cooperation with Trout Unlimited, the Pennsylvania Fish and Boat Commission, and many other supporting groups. Now in its third year, the program allows 30 to 40 high school leaders to participate in a weeklong workshop held in late June at Allenberry Resort in Boiling Springs. The ultimate goal for these youngsters is to educate them in water conservation. Tomorrow's leader will be well grounded in entomology, hydrology, geology, and, of course, fly-fishing and fly-tying. Just think—in 10 years this camp will have affected 300 to 400 of our future leaders. Not a bad start! You can contact this group at Trout Unlimited, Box 520, Carlisle, PA 17013.

The Fly Fishers Apprentice Program in Ithaca, New York, is another worthwhile project aimed at working with our youth and teaching them fly-fishing skills. Headed by Phil Genova and Paul Roberts, this project is sponsored by the Cooperative Extension and the Sportfishing and Aquatic Resource Education Program at Cornell University. Youngsters learn fly-fishing and fly-tying—and much more. Many of the students in the program agree that it has motivated them in high school as well. The next step for this organization is the formation of a retail fly shop in Ithaca. There's no shop within miles of this college town; opening one will give youngsters in the program a chance to learn the finer details of running a business. You can contact them at Fly Fishers Apprentice Program, 407 West Seneca Street, Ithaca, NY 14850.

Frank Burt Smoot lives in Pikesville, Maryland. He's a noted illustrator, artist, conservationist, and fly-fisher. The prestigious Potomac Valley Fly Fishers of Frederick recently made him a lifetime member of their club. Frank takes little credit for the work he's done; often he identifies other people, insisting that he didn't do it single-handedly. But he has devoted more than six decades to conservation—much of that with youngsters. He's worked with thousands of youths in 4-H, the Brotherhood of the

A brown trout caught on a Patriot

Jungle Cock, and other organizations teaching them conservation and fly-fishing. Frank is 90 years young and deserves all the credit he gets.

"The most precious resource in the United States is our youth," says Frank, when he's asked why he continues to teach conservation classes.

Recently Frank received a proclamation from the governor and the senate of Maryland, recognizing his work in conservation and with the youth of the state.

These are just a few of the organizations and people working with youngsters today. The ultimate goal of all of these projects is to develop an acute awareness and love of the outdoors and of how it can be conserved, preserved, and enjoyed by future generations.

Index

ALSO FROM THE COUNTRYMAN PRESS AND BACKCOUNTRY PUBLICATIONS